Science

Project

Helper

Science Project Helper

MIKE DICKINSON

*Equipped with his five senses, man explores the
universe around him and calls the adventure Science.*

– Edwin Powell Hubble

Illustrated by
Carolyn Gill

San Antonio, Texas
2006

Science Project Helper © 2006
by Mike Dickinson

Drawings by Carolyn Gill. Cover illustration taken from the science fair journal of Michael
Milligan, 1996. Used by permission.

Updates and other useful information related to
Science Project Helper may be found at
http://www.scienceprojecthelper.com

First Edition

ISBN-13: 978-0-930324-77-3
ISBN-10: 0-930324-77-3
(paperback original)

Wings Press
627 E. Guenther
San Antonio, Texas 78210
Phone/fax: (210) 271-7805
On-line catalogue and ordering:
www.wingspress.com

Library of Congress Cataloging-in-Publication data:

Dickinson, Mike
    Science project helper / Mike Dickinson ; illustrated by Carolyn Gill.
        p. cm.
    Includes bibliographical references.
    ISBN 0-930324-77-3 / 978-0-930324-77-3 (alk. paper)
[1.Science projects—Juvenile literature. 2. Science—Experiments—Juvenile literature.
3. Science—Study and teaching—Juvenile literature.] I. Title.

    Q182.3 .D52 2006
        507.8—dc21   Cataloging by St. Philip's College

About the Author

Mike Dickinson got sidetracked with the gadgetry in his high school science
project and never looked back. Later, he helped his college professors conduct research on water cycles and radiation safety practices while earning a
B.S. degree in Physical Science. As an instructor pilot he survived many
student pilots' hypotheses about how man can fly. He uses his Masters
degrees in business and educational technology as an instructional designer
and corporate training director. He is passionate about removing the
shroud of mystery that often surrounds complex tasks by breaking them
down into bite-size chunks and providing clear explanations. He and his
wife, herself a science teacher, enjoy their two daughters and their families.

TABLE OF CONTENTS

Appendices:

Science Project Helper is dedicated to my grandchildren,
Kaitlyn, Josh and Olivia,
whose sense of wonder and imagination are a constant sense of renewal.
Who knows what you will learn and discover? Enjoy your own journey!

You can teach a student a lesson for a day;
but if you can teach him to learn by creating curiosity,
he will continue the learning process as long as he lives.

– Clay P. Bedford

From the Publisher:

Wings Press has been called "the best little publishing house in Texas," and its books and authors have won numerous awards – but the reputation of this press and its authors lies exclusively in the realm of literature, not science or education. So why has Wings elected to publish a book dedicated to science projects? Two reasons, really: one is philosophical, regarding the relationship between truth and beauty; the other is personal, based on fifteen years of experience with my own children competing in local, regional, state, and international science fairs.

Thoughtful people throughout the course of human history have spent a lot of time considering the nature of beauty, and if there is any consensus, it comes to this: beauty resides in harmonious relationships. In an earlier time, it was traditional to say that no one knew more about beauty than poets, but who actually investigates "harmonious relationships" more deeply than scientists and mathematicians? As Leon Lederman put it in his book, *The God Particle*, "In our telescopes and microscopes, in our observatories and laboratories – and on our notepads – we begin to perceive the outlines of the pristine beauty and symmetry that governed the first moments of the universe. We can almost see it."

As in so many situations where humanity has found ways to divide itself into separate camps, the divide between humanists and scientists is mainly one of language. But to those who are truly bilingual in what C.P. Snow termed "the two cultures" of the sciences and the humanities – those who read the calculus as easily as they read a novel – there is a way of seeing that the artist and the scientist, no matter their individual disciplines, are really looking for the same thing. Thus there is a way of seeing Einstein's field equations as a deeply metaphoric type of poetry just as there is a way of seeing a mathematical basis for the artistic use of words or a paintbrush or a chisel or notes on a staff. Many great scientists have seen this and written about it, including Einstein, Lederman, Loren Eiseley, Stephen Hawking, and others.

So where does truth come in? I would quote a poet on this: "Beauty is truth, truth beauty. That is all ye know, and all ye need to know." John Keats said that. Keats was saying that the pursuit of knowledge and understanding is one more way to pursue beauty, to seek out those harmonious relationships upon which the existence of the very universe depends. That seems sufficient reason for a literary publishing house to promote education in the sciences.

On the personal level, my son and daughter, Michael and Brigid, both competed in science fairs from kindergarten through their senior years in high school. They did many fascinating experiments, and – with the supervision of some amazingly generous mentors – ended up doing some significant original research. It involved a good deal of hard work, but all along the way we had a lot of sheer fun. The pursuit of understanding how something worked in several diverse fields required them to learn about new topics not as abstract concepts, but as practical tools. They were not "driven" to this by their parents, teachers, or mentors, but they *were* driven – by the love of knowledge and, frankly, by the thrill of both the pursuit and the competitive drama.

Like many other "science fair kids," they both earned full scholarships for college, which was a direct result of the kind of education they acquired by doing research and experimentation for their science fair projects, and from the experience of presenting their research with confidence, style, and enthusiasm. Their parents, a writer and a librarian, are eternally grateful for that experience, which gave our children so much more than we could provide as individuals and more than their schools could provide in the classroom, although they had some stellar science teachers along the way. Mike Dickinson has acknowledged several people in his life who played a role in the development of this book. From the publisher's perspective, I would like to dedicate it to Brigid and Michael, and to the mentors who gave so freely of their time, Moises Sandoval and James Frazer, Ph.D.

– Bryce Milligan
Publisher, Wings Press

Acknowledgments:

Several people led to my writing this book. My interest in science was kindled by several science teachers from middle school through college. I appreciated their knowledge, experiments, and counsel. The precipitating event behind this book was my wife Marilyn's enthusiasm for teaching science together with her compassion for students and parents whose unfamiliarity with the science project process too often obscured the joy of discovery.

Others helped with the book itself. My publisher, Bryce Milligan, encouraged me throughout. Several science teachers shared from their experience: Mary Poarch, Shawnee Friend, Mike Brown, Ken Newkirk, Jenny Tice, Mary Jeter, Bob Dougherty, Bob Berger, Ph.D., and John Prince, PhD. Michele Glidden at Science Service shared insights from her unique vantage point at the agency that runs the national-level science and engineering fairs.

Several students contributed, too. Projects by Austin Jeter, Marisa Luckie, Hailey Pulman, Camden Mahbubani, all from Keystone School of San Antonio, and others helped me refine my concepts and descriptions. The work of two students and insights from their parents became integral parts of the book: Amy Robinson and Nick Berger.

John Day, Ph.D., "Cloudman," has been a life-long friend and mentor, from many hours years ago discussing his cloud physics research and using photographs to collect and analyze data, up through the present with his critique of the book. Others who helped improve the initial manuscript are Jim Larson, Ph.D., Steven Jacobs, and James Fraser, Ph.D. A big thank you to Leon Lederman, Ph.D., for his exceptional and – to me – totally unexpected "blurb" for the back of the book.

Thank you, each of you, for being so forthcoming with your help and for entrusting me to blend your stories in a way that can help others enjoy the pursuit of new knowledge.

Introduction

This book will take you from "Oh my gosh – a science project," to finished display, step by step, in just a few weeks. It will provide the help you need whether your goal is survival, a blue ribbon, or even a scholarship.

What is a science project?

A science project is really a process that consists of these six steps:

1. Choose your topic and question.

2. Develop your hypothesis (educated guess as to the answer to your question).

3. Plan how you'll conduct your project.

4. Carry out your plan.

5. Interpret your results.

6. Communicate your results to others.

This six-step process is known as the scientific method. It is used by scientists doing research around the world. It can even help in your daily life, as you'll see in Chapter 11.

How will this book help you?

Science Project Helper shows exactly what you have to do in each step and what the outcome should be. It offers clear tips and examples along the way. Most importantly, it provides unique HELPERS throughout the process to guide you through the thinking process.

Ready to begin? Let's go!

First Things First

The very first thing you should do is to buy a three-section spiral notebook. This will be your project journal. Here's what each section is for:

1. Notes about your topic and background information (see Chapters 1 and 2).

2. Thoughts and notes as you design your experiment and collect data (see Chapters 3 and 4).

3. Analysis of your data, conclusions, and outline of your research report (see Chapters 5 and 6).

Science Project Helper

A Word About Science Fairs . . .

If you're holding this book because you or someone you love has just been assigned their first science project, not to worry. Your teacher will explain the process that you're to follow at your school. This always includes some form of teacher approval before you actually start gathering data. It may also require other approvals depending on the topic and method you choose to follow. Many schools use the same approval forms used by national science fairs, so those forms and processes are referred to in various places in the book.

There are two major science fairs in the United States at the national level, one for middle school and one for high school:

- The Discovery Channel Young Scientist Challenge, or DCYSC, is for students in grades 5 through 8.

- The Intel International Science and Engineering Fair, or ISEF, is for high school students, grades 9 through 12.

If you're fortunate enough to win a top place at your school's science fair you may be asked to go on to regional or state competition. You will be told which forms to use and the entry process to follow. Usually that will be DCYSC forms for middle school and ISEF forms for high school. Some schools or states are not affiliated with DCYSC or ISEF, so they may use slightly different rules and approval processes. Again, your teacher will know the process you must follow.

Just so you can see what they look like, there is a complete set of ISEF approval forms for the 2006-2007 school year in Appendix B. Always check the DCYSC or ISEF web site for the current forms and entry process.

See p. 81 for the web address for DCYSC and ISEF, and for information on entering science fairs.

So where does *Science Project Helper* come in? As you saw on the preceding page, Science Project Helper leads you step-by-step through a process known as the scientific method. Science Project Helper helps you design and conduct your experiment; DCYSC and ISEF provide the rules and approval forms so science fair competitions will be fair.

The history of science has many heroes, both experimenters and theorists. The Greek mathematician Archimedes (287-212 BC) was known for his discoveries in mechanics and hydrostatics. His invention for raising water from one level to another, called the "Archimedean screw," is still used in rural communities all over the world to help irrigate crops. Sir Isaac Newton lived in England (1642-1727). He developed theories of universal gravitation and terrestrial mechanics, discovered the diffraction of light and invented an entire branch of mathematics, the differential calculus.

Chapter 1

Somewhere, something fantastic is waiting to be known.
– Carl Sagan

Step 1: Choose your topic and question

Chapter preview	
Sub-steps:	a. Find a topic b. Gather background information c. Pick a question (but not just any question) d. Be aware of project types
What happens in this step:	In Step 1 you pick a topic and learn enough about it so you can identify the question you want to explore in your science project.
Time to allow:	Two days to two weeks

Overview of Step 1

The key to a fun, successful science project is to find just the right topic and question. You want a question that you are interested in and that's not too easy or hard for you to answer. This chapter will help you find that question.

Step 1a – Find a topic

This section will help you find a topic that's interesting to you.

Journal note: As you go through this chapter, write down topics, ideas, and questions you come up with. Use section 1 of your 3-part journal. Keep it with you at all times. Sometimes a great question will just pop into your head, but later it's hard to remember. And that might have been the topic or question that would make a great science project.

a. Use the N.O.W. technique

1. **Notice** things around you:
   - Pay more attention to things you usually don't stop to notice.
   - Maybe you notice something and wonder what it is or why it works or looks the way it does.
2. **Observe:**
   - Look closely at how things look, listen carefully to the sounds they make, observe how they move or change.
   - Do you see any causes-and-effects that raise questions in your mind?

3. <u>**Wonder:**</u>

> *Men love to wonder, and that is the seed of science.*
> – Ralph Waldo Emerson

> *Millions saw the apple fall, but Newton asked why.*
> – Bernard Baruch

- Ask yourself, "I wonder why something works the way it does?" or "I wonder what would happen if…"

- As you wonder, your questions might start becoming specific, like these:

  o I wonder which makes a baseball go farther, a wooden bat or an aluminum one?
  o Which plants in my yard seem to attract the most butterflies? I wonder why?

☞   Camden noticed a TV ad about a certain detergent's cleaning power. She observed the detergent her mom used – and how it seemed to clean the clothes – and wondered, "Which one really is the best?" You guessed it: she had her question!

☞   Many years ago a 17-year old boy noticed a chandelier that was swinging in his church. He observed it for awhile; it seemed to keep the same time whether swinging lightly or much more broadly depending on the strength of the breeze hitting it. He wondered if he was correct, so he did more studies under controlled conditions. Sure enough! That was in 1581. The boy's name was Galileo, he was in the Cathedral of Pisa, and that's how he discovered the principle of the pendulum.

b. Use the topic HELPER

Use the form on the next two pages to help you think of *things you are interested in.* Discuss the questions with your parent or teacher to help you clarify your answers. Think of answers that might spark a science project idea. Remember to write your answers and thoughts in your project journal.

TOPIC HELPER

This is not a test. There are no right or wrong answers. Do your best to answer these questions the way you feel. You don't have to answer all of them, only the ones that catch your interest. When you think you've found your topic, go on to section 1b (gather background information).

Journal note: As you get ideas from this HELPER, make a note of them in your journal, even if they seem zany or too simple at the time. Your subconscious mind will work on them like a piece of clay and – who knows – you might come up with just the right question in a day or two.

1. List two of your favorite activities after school:

    •

    •

2. List two sports or hobbies that you like:

    •

    •

3. Think about your answers above, and ask yourself: "Are there some questions that would be interesting to explore – or that I've been wondering about?"

    ☞ Nick loved playing baseball. He had used some aluminum bats and liked the way they felt. Some of his friends liked them, too, but others still preferred wooden bats. Nick wondered if he could devise a test to see which kind of bat really hit the ball farthest.

4. Ask your teacher for help. Your teacher already knows you and your interests and can often suggest some topics he or she knows you'd be interested in.

    ☞ Marisa L. talked with her science teacher to get her general idea. She wondered what effect radiation has on the growth of radish seeds. But when she read more about it, she discovered that the idea was too popular. She decided to study how radiation slows the growth of radish seeds.

5. Do you know what job you want to do when you grow up? Write it down. Are you curious about anything related to this job? Write that, too.

6. Is there something about one of your parents' jobs or hobbies that may provide an interesting question?

7. Could you explore any issues in the news? Watch channels like your local news or Discovery Channel. Read your local paper. What's going on with the local environment? Check out this web site called "The Why Files: science behind the news:" http://whyfiles.org/ Has anyone made a claim about one of these issues that you could test to see if it's true? Where can you find out more about these issues?

    ☞ Brigid noticed newscasts about a local water issue. Citizens were complaining that a catfish farmer was polluting the water that went downstream. He claimed innocence, saying he used special food so that the fish waste contained no fecal coliform bacteria. Brigid wanted to find out whose claims were true. She wondered if she could get some catfish and feed them the same food as that man, to see if the fish waste was polluting the river.

8. Do you have any collections?

9. Have you seen any claims on TV that you would like to test?

☞   Camden M. got her idea from claims she saw in a TV commercial about a certain detergent's cleaning power.

10. Do you know someone in a science-related profession like a doctor, scientist, or laboratory worker?

☞   Hailey P. got her idea from her aunt, a doctor, who got her wondering about bacteria levels in local drinking fountains.

☞   Austin J's parents were close friends with a dentist, with whom they got together frequently. Austin asked him for ideas, and settled on examining the staining effects of different drinks on teeth enamel.

11. Have you seen a gadget or instrument that you would like to work with? Or a model of something? Can you get one? Can you think of a way to use it to explore an interesting question?

12. If by now you have a topic that you like, go on to Step 1b. Otherwise, try the next ways of finding a topic.

c. Scan lists of topics or projects.

Another way to find a topic is to shop around. There are lots of books and web sites with lists of topics. Caution: These lists can be a good source of ideas, but be sure you figure out your own research question. You can build on what someone else did – that's good science – but be careful not to merely repeat someone else's experiment. That would not be ethical.

If you get ideas from someone else's work, be sure to give them proper credit. You do this in your bibliography (for written sources such as books and the internet) or acknowledgements (for people who helped you in person). Notice how those two sections are used in this book.

Note the list of sample topics organized by science fair category in Appendix A. Maybe that will be enough to give you an idea.

Books: Look through other science project books, some of which list lots of project ideas. See what's available in your library or local bookstore, or on online bookstores such as Amazon.com, Borders.com, or Barnesandnoble.com. Chapter 9 lists several books that might be helpful.

Internet:

a. Use terms like these in the search window of your internet software. Note: to search for exact phrases, put them in quotes like you see here:

   i. "science project" and "topic"
   ii. "science project" and "middle school"
   iii. "science project" and "idea" or "hypothesis"
   iv. substitute "science fair" in place of "science project" above

b. Here are two links to get you started:

    1. http://www.all-science-fair-projects.com
    2. http://school.discovery.com/sciencefaircentral/ Click on Project Ideas.

c. There are other internet links in Chapter 9.

Step 1b: Gather background information

You need to find out what is already known about your topic. Then you can think of a question that either expands that knowledge or applies it to a specific situation. Don't worry: there are plenty of questions you can explore. They're all around you once you know what to look for, just like the students whose ideas you saw in the Topic HELPER.

For example, you might have read that ants can carry several times their weight. That would be considered common knowledge. But think about this: *what* do the ants on *your* sidewalk carry? That would be something new that you could learn through your project.

Or, how far do *your* team mates hit a baseball with a wood vs. aluminum bat? You could find out what the pros do through the library or internet, but it would take your project to know about your own team.

    ☞ Amy was looking through her family's books on science projects from when her sister did her project. A project on stopping milk from spoiling caught her interest. She wanted to see about keeping some other kind of food fresh. Since she likes bananas so well, and they don't stay fresh long, she wanted to investigate that. In her reading, she learned about enzymes and the role they play in food spoilage. She learned that enzymes may be affected by temperature and exposure to the air, so Amy now had some ideas for her question.

Parent tip: Perhaps the most important time you can help your young scientist is when they're figuring out their topic and question and gathering background information. You can help them think of places to find information. Take them to the library. Bounce ideas around to help your child mold them into a question they really want to explore. Perhaps you can also suggest where and how they might find an expert on their chosen topic to get some technical advice if they need it.

    ☞ Emily R. wanted to use small colored candies in her project, which led her initially to the topic of color separation. But her mother urged her to "do something more serious." Emily settled on the topic called "Healing Touch," because her mother, a nurse, was watching a videotape on this topic at the time. Emily was 9 years old when this happened, and her experiment went on to be one of the most famous science projects in recent years, even being written up in a national magazine and reported on CNN!

GATHERING-BACKGROUND-INFORMATION HELPER

Here are some tips to help you find background information and to know what to look for.

1. Try the library.

    a. Ask the librarian to help you. They're in that profession because they love helping people find information. So let your librarian help you!

    b. Search for books by topic in the library's catalog.

    c. Look through scientific magazines like Discover; National Geographic Kids; National Geographic World; Odyssey: Adventures in Science; Popular Science; Ranger Rick; and U.S. Kids.

    d. Browse books on the shelves.

        i. Start by looking up your topic in encyclopedias. They're a great place to get concise explanations.

        ii. If your library uses the Dewey Decimal system, check out these areas in the Juvenile book section (or the adult section if you're in high school):

            1. Basic science is in all of the 500's

                a. Science project books are usually numbered 507.8

                b. Science experiments for children are numbered 507.2

                c. Find the section in the 500's that has books on your specific topic, too.

            2. Applied science (technology) is in the 600's. For example,

                a. Medical science is in the 610's

                b. Agriculture is in the 630's

                c. Chemical engineering is in the 660's

        iii. If your library uses the Library of Congress cataloguing system, Science is in the Q section, and books on science projects are mainly at Q175.2.M66.

        iv. If you live in a remote area, you might search for books at the Library of Congress's web site, and then use Interlibrary Loan through your closest library.

Library of Congress website:

http://catalog.loc.gov/cgi-bin/Pwebrecon.cgi?DB=local&PAGE=First

2. Try the internet. You can do this at home or at the library. Libraries usually subscribe to data bases that you can't tap into from home. Just as with books, ask your librarian to help you plan your search.

3. With the library and the internet, **use a variety of search words** related to your topic. What could you try for the baseball question? You could try baseball, batting averages, physics, and similar terms. How about for the banana question? Try banana, fruit, freshness, food, food storage, and enzymes.

4. Keep notes in your journal. You don't have to summarize whole articles. Do jot down key information and the source where you found it. Also jot down other ideas that come to you during this process. One of those ideas may be just what you need for a great project, and you might not remember it later.

5. Keep track of your sources. When you're first finding information it's easy to lose track of where you found what. Try these tips:

a. While you're in the middle of your search, jot down at least the book or magazine title (and article title), author, and date.

b. For internet sites, jot down the web address (URL), or cut and paste addresses into a word processing document that you can save and print out. Remember this advice, because you can get to clicking from one site to another and lose total track of where you found that one key piece of information. You can also print out web pages.

6. What should you be trying to find out? Here are some questions to guide your information-gathering:

a. What is already known about this topic?

b. Are there any commonly accepted principles or scientific laws that relate to your topic or question? (Even if it isn't labeled that way, if you see the same thing described in two or three places, that's probably a commonly accepted principle.)

c. What questions have other people addressed?

d. Has anyone addressed a question similar to the one you're interested in? If so, how did they approach it? Might your result be the same, or different? Why?

7. When do you have enough background information? When you know enough to have a decent science project question and you can make an educated guess as to its outcome. Not a perfect guess; an educated one. This usually requires at least three to six different sources.

8. Your information-gathering may change your choice of topic. That's okay. You may find a topic with a better question than the first one you picked. Go for it!

9. You may need an expert. Sometimes you just can't find out all you need to know from written sources. Or, let's face it; it's easier to ask someone than look it up! If you need an expert's advice, write down the questions you want to ask them. Then ask your teacher and

parents where you might find someone who could address your questions. Be prepared: they'll
see immediately if you've gathered good background information and will be all the more will-
ing to help you.

Step 1c: Pick a question (but not just any question)

> *The scientist is not a person who gives the right answers,*
> *he's one who asks the right questions.*
> — Claude Lévi-Strauss, *Le Cru et le cuit*, 1964

> *My mother made me a scientist without ever intending to. Every other Jewish mother in*
> *Brooklyn would ask her child after school, "So? Did you learn anything today?" But not*
> *my mother. "Izzy," she would say, "did you ask a good question today?" That*
> *difference – asking good questions - made me become a scientist.*
> — Isidor Isaac Rabi

Somewhere through the process of choosing a topic and gathering background information you will form questions in your mind. Write those questions in your journal. Then narrow them down to the one you want to pursue for this project.

Scientists use three main questions to guide their research. Keep these in mind as you
search for your topic:

1. What is it?

2. How does it work?

3. Why does it work that way?

What makes a good science project question? Not just any old question. You don't want
a question that's already common knowledge, and you don't want one that's going to be impossible to answer. You want one that's just right.

So what is a question that's just right?

"Select an interesting topic that will produce a measurable experiment with easy to obtain
equipment," says Mr. Mike Brown, a science teacher at Selah Middle School in Washington
State. He goes on to say, "Don't pick a topic that requires equipment you cannot build, bor-
row or use."[1]

You may not fully know all the equipment you will need for your project until you complete the next two chapters. So if you have a really keen idea now but don't know how you'll
get the equipment you need, don't give up yet. Other kids have come up with some pretty ingen-
ious devices. You can see one example on pages 56 and 57.

---

1. Brown, Mike, "How to use this model project journal," [Online]
http://www.selah.wednet.edu/JHS/Brown/SMSProjJourn.html#topofjournal, circa 1999. Used with permission.

Take some care in choosing the question or problem that your science project will focus on. Your goal is to learn something that is not known, at least in your particular situation, or to verify something you think will happen. If someone, somewhere, may know the likely outcome (including your teacher), that's okay. What matters is that you don't know the answer (yet), but you can design and conduct an experiment that will provide an answer.

This is a good place to get your teacher's advice. He or she can recognize the overall scope of your question and tell whether it's feasible or not. Your teacher can also suggest ways to modify a too-difficult question to make it do-able.

Science Fair tip: Check out the EnergyQuest web site, What Makes a Good Science Project? It offers good tips and ideas. http://www.energyquest.ca.gov/projects/advice.html

Step 1d: - Be aware of project types

There are different types of science projects, and some are better choices than others.

One type is called **Descriptive** or **Observation**. This answers that first question that scientists ask: *What is it?* Like the name implies, this type of project mainly involves describing something, often something you observe. For example, a girl once did a marvelous study of an island at the Oregon Coast where she identified and catalogued all the creatures that lived on the island. No one had ever done that before. Some students choose a scientific principle or model, then build a display that illustrates it. This may be okay for your very first project, but unless you can use the model to test a hypothesis (see Chapter 2), you really aren't setting up an experiment, and that's what science projects are mainly about. Here is a web site with lots of hands on activities: http://www.ycsmag.bc.ca/projects/projects.html Maybe you can develop a question or hypothesis that uses one of these activities.

As opposed to descriptive projects, **experiments** attempt to learn about relationships between two things, like Amy's air temperature and banana freshness. Experiments help answer scientists' other two questions: *How* does it work (what is the relationship), and *why* does it work that way? It's much easier to show *how* something works than *why*. For example, we're going to see Nick's experiment later where he wanted to see which bat people could hit a baseball farther with, aluminum or wood. Nick did find a relationship between bat material and how far the ball was hit. That was enough for a good experiment. But wouldn't you agree that figuring out *why* one bat hit farther could be a lot harder? Interesting, but harder.

If you choose to do a descriptive experiment, some parts of this book will still be helpful, like gathering background information and getting ready to present your project verbally. But the book's main focus is how to do original experiments for a science project.

CHAPTER SUMMARY

Step 1: Choose your topic and question	
Purpose of this step	In Step 1 you pick a topic and learn enough about it so you can identify the question you want to explore in your science project.
Sub-steps	a. Find a topic b. Gather background information c. Pick a question (but not just any question) d. Be aware of project types
Tips	• Choose a topic that interests *you*. • Read all you can find about your topic. • Develop the main question you want to pursue.
Tools	Use the N.O.W. technique (p. 3) and Use the Topic HELPER (pp. 4-6)
Traps	Avoid questions that are common knowledge. Warning: if you want to use people, hazardous materials, or vertebrate animals (those with backbones) in your project, you will need special permission. This will be covered in Step 3d.
The finer points	If your topic is about plants, here's a word of caution: it takes several weeks to grow and study plants, and they may be subject to a lot of conditions out of your control: weather, insects, poor seed. You can do an experiment using plants, just be aware that these projects require extra care when setting them up.

Chapter 2

Step 2: Develop Your Hypothesis

Chapter preview	
Sub-steps:	None for this step
What happens in this step:	Use your question and background information to make an educated guess about a possible outcome to your question. This guess is called your hypothesis. It serves as the bridge between Step 1 and the entire rest of your project.
Time to allow:	You may find you need to modify your question or gather more background information before you can settle on your hypothesis. Thus, this step could take anywhere from one or two days to a couple of weeks.

What is a hypothesis, anyway?

Your hypothesis is *the most important part of your whole science project*. **The** most important. Your hypothesis will be the bridge between everything you've done on your science project up to this point, and everything you'll do from here on out.

Here's a definition: A hypothesis is a one-sentence statement of a possible outcome to a question or problem. You will design your project to see if that outcome really happens. That's why the hypothesis is a bridge. It takes you from Step 1 to the entire rest of your project. It is a powerful statement, so take care in crafting it.

Examples

Let's look at some examples to see what this all means, and then you can develop the hypothesis for your project.

Ever been fishing? If you chose a certain spot because you just knew that's where the fish would be, you made a hypothesis. Even if you weren't 100% certain, if you chose a fishing hole based on the layout of the river's bank, the depth of the water, vegetation, or whatever, you made a hypothesis. It went something like this: If fish hang out where there's lots of yucky vegetation underwater, then I'll surely catch some fish in this spot. You tested that hypothesis, too. Catch any fish?

Here are some other examples of hypotheses:

1. Chocolate may cause pimples.
2. Plants may grow faster if the temperature is warmer.
3. Music may affect people's moods.
4. Some herbs may preserve food.

Notice that each statement above states a possible relationship between one thing and another.

Chocolate   ➔   pimples
Temperature   ➔   plant growth
Music   ➔   moods

From your own knowledge you know that each of these effects *could* happen. In your science project you'll set up a test to see if such an outcome actually *does* happen. Scientists do this under controlled conditions. That way they know that whatever happens to the second thing – called the responding variable -- could *only* happen from the change in the first thing. Generally your experience alone isn't enough to go on, so that's why it was so important to collect background information in Step 1.

☞ Aristotle thought that the speed of falling objects depended on their weight. He and others based this belief on simple observations and logic. Later, Galileo performed detailed experiments and found this was only true for very light or very heavy objects. Galileo's experiments were so detailed that he developed ways to predict the path of things like cannonballs using mathematics. Ever since that time, 1589, scientists have relied on experiments to check their reasoning.

Who else makes hypotheses? Lots of people, everyday. Take doctors, for instance. Doctors don't say it exactly this way, but here's the thinking they use: "If your symptoms are due to the flu, then this medicine will help you feel better in a day." Just like the fishing example, this hypothesis gets tested, too. Did you feel better in a day? Hope so! But that wasn't a guaranteed outcome; it was an educated guess which could prove correct, or not correct. That's how a hypothesis works.

Some things are predictions, not hypotheses. If you say "I'm going to score 95% on the next exam," that's a prediction – a simple statement of an outcome. But if you say, "If I focus my studying on X, Y, and Z, then I'll score 95% on the exam," that's a hypothesis, because it states the expected *effect* of one variable (your studying) on another (your test score).

Who made these hypotheses?

Some famous people have made hypotheses that had huge impact. Who made these hypotheses?

   • If the world is round instead of flat, then I can reach India by sailing west from Spain instead of east.

   • If we devote enough effort and money to it, we can put a man on the moon by the end of the decade [1960's].

Your hypothesis probably won't lead to a long voyage or a trip to the moon, so relax -- you won't have to drum up millions of dollars (in case you were wondering). But your hypothesis will set the course of events for you and others for the next several weeks, just like it did for these two men and the people they affected.

How do I develop my hypothesis?

Why such a big deal about a hypothesis? This: You may hear or believe something is true, or you may just wonder if something is true. The only way to know for sure is to test it. A well-written hypothesis enables you to set up a valid test. So take some care in writing your hypothesis and the rest of your science project will follow smoothly.

I have no special talents. I am only passionately curious.
~ Albert Einstein

How do you go about developing your hypothesis? The Hypothesis HELPER will lead you through the process. Make sure your teacher approves your hypothesis before you go further with your project.

HYPOTHESIS HELPER

1. Write your final question from Step 1c here. (Example: which storage method will keep bananas fresh longer?)

2. List three to six key things you already know about your topic and question:

i. _____

ii. _____

iii. _____

iv. _____

v. _____

vi. _____

Examples:

- Bananas don't stay fresh very long
- Enzymes cause bananas to ripen
- Enzymes' action may be slowed in the absence of air
- Enzymes' action is a lot slower at lower temperatures

3. Using what you know from your background information, follow these steps to restate your question from Step 1 as a hypothesis:

i. You can first write your hypothesis like some of the examples above, as "may" statements. E.g., chocolate may cause pimples.

_____

_____

ii. A better way to state a hypothesis so you can test it is to use an **If-then** format. For example, *if* chocolate causes pimples, *then* kids who eat more chocolate will get more pimples. Here's another example: *If* air and warmer temperatures speed up the ripening of bananas, *then* bananas in zip-lock bags at room temperature will ripen faster but stay fresh longer than open air or refrigerated storage.

iii. Now write your hypothesis as an **If-then statement** (use pencil; sometimes it takes a time or two to get the words just right):

If _____

_____

then _____

_____ .

4. Have your teacher or parent go over your hypothesis with you. It should be worded so that the second variable depends on what happens to the first. This is why the If-then format is so important. Using the previous examples:

i. If chocolate causes pimples, then eating more chocolate will cause kids to break out more.

ii. If temperature and air affect banana freshness, then they should stay fresh longer if they're stored in sealed plastic bags.

The first variable is called the *manipulated*[2] variable. You are going to set up your experiment to control how that variable...varies! The second variable is called the *responding* variable. Your experiment will measure the changes in the responding variable, and then you'll know if your hypothesis was correct or not.

Note: The important thing about your hypothesis is *not* whether it turns out as you predicted. The important thing is that you design an experiment that is a valid test of the relationship between those two variables. Your hypothesis serves as a "target" around which to design your experiment, or test.

5. Speaking of tests, make sure your hypothesis is a SMART one. When you read it, does it seem:

i. **S**pecific (what are the variables, exactly?)

ii. **M**easurable (will you be able to measure both variables?)

iii. **A**ttainable (will you be able to get the materials and equipment needed to control and test the variables?)

iv. **R**ealistic (does your hypothesis state a plausible outcome?)

v. **T**imed (will you be able to set up your experiment and get measurable results in the time available?)

Your teacher should check your hypothesis to see if it's doable. Once you get the okay, then the hardest part of your project is behind you. Congratulations! Now you're ready to design your experiment.

---

2. There are two sets of terms used for these variables. In this book we'll use "manipulated" and "responding" since they describe the relationship vividly. However, in strict scientific lingo – and on many state achievement tests – they are called "independent" (for manipulated) and "dependent" (for responding).

CHAPTER SUMMARY

Chapter 2 – Step 2: Develop your hypothesis	
Purpose of this step	Using your question and background information from Step 1, develop your hypothesis (educated guess)
Sub-steps	None

Tips	• State your hypothesis in If-then format
	• Make your hypothesis SMART
	    ○ Specific
	    ○ Measurable
	    ○ Attainable
	    ○ Realistic
	    ○ Timed

Tools	Hypothesis HELPER
Traps	Don't just state a prediction

Chapter 3

An experiment is a question which science poses to Nature, and a measurement is the recording of Nature's answer.
— Max Planck, Scientific Autobiography and Other Papers, 1949

Step 3 – Plan how you'll conduct your experiment

Chapter preview	
Sub-steps:	a. Identify variables and controls b. Develop your plan c. List and obtain materials and equipment d. Get approval
What happens in this step:	You will need to gather data under controlled conditions to test your hypothesis. In Step 3 you plan the way you'll gather that data. You'll figure out the exact steps to follow and write them down. You will also figure out what material or equipment you'll need in order to do your experiment. **Caution:** <u>You must get the approval of your teacher</u> and, in some cases, other adults <u>before</u> you actually start doing your experiment. This will ensure your safety and that of others. Step 3d explains how to get approval.
Time to allow:	Two to three days. Longer if you need to test run certain parts of your procedures. You may also need time to get or make equipment.

Please note: the two to three days is *planning* time – not the time you'll need to conduct your actual experiment.

Have you ever made something without following the instructions? Maybe you got lucky and figured it out. With a science project, you must develop a plan before you start. Safety needs to be built in. And you need accurate procedures – in advance – so your data and conclusions are valid. Sometimes a great idea about one part of your project will come to you while you are working on another one. So allow plenty of time for planning and keep your notes!

Step 3a: Identify variables and controls

Remember Nick's variables? In scientific terms, the bat material is called his *manipulated* variable (wood vs. aluminum). How far the ball went is called his *responding* variable. To keep these terms straight, think of it this way:

- When you *manipulate* something, you change it on purpose. What Nick changed was the bat material: wood or aluminum.

- A hypothesis states how we think the other variable will *respond* to the changes. So in Nick's project the responding variable was the distance the ball flew.

Now it gets interesting, because other things could affect a ball's distance too. Right? Things like wind, kind of ball, how the ball was pitched, and how hard the ball is hit, could all affect distance. Here's a little table that shows these things for Nick's project:

Project/Question	Manipulated variable (Input)	Responding Variable (Outcome)	Other variables that could affect the responding variable
1. Which baseball bat hits farther?	Bat material (wood or aluminum)	Distance ball travels	• Kind of ball • Weight of bat • Weather • Batter fatigue • How ball is pitched

If those other things in the last column *do* vary, then more than one thing would affect the outcome. Nick still wouldn't know the effect of wooden or aluminum bats on ball distance.

Those other things are also called variables (just plain variables). Nick and you and all scientists have the same challenge. That is, set up the experiment so these other variables have little effect on the responding variable. This is called *controlling*.

Let's see how this works. Look at the variable about how the ball is pitched. Hmmm, that could make a big difference in how cleanly the ball is hit and thus how far it flies. Who can pitch a ball exactly the same way every time? One way to *control* that would be with a pitching machine. Could Nick find one to use? If not, what could he do instead? As it turns out, Nick just had each batter toss the ball up and hit it themselves.

Another variable is batter fatigue. If all the batters hit several balls with one bat, then switch and hit several with the other bat, they'd be more tired when using the second bat. Nick could have them hit with one bat one day, then come back the next day and hit with the other bat. That would work. But he decided to just have them switch bats on each hit. So they'd go back and forth, wood, aluminum, wood, aluminum.

Can you see why a plan is so important? Could Nick just take some friends out to the ballpark and let 'em hit away? That wouldn't control his variables very well, would it?

This table shows variables for the students' projects used in the Topic HELPER. You can trace the thinking process in identifying variables.

Project/Question	Manipulated variable (Input)	Responding Variable (Outcome)	Other variables that could affect the responding variable
1. What's the best way to keep bananas fresh?	Temperature and amount of air	Freshness	• Ripeness at the beginning • Amount of light
2. Which drinking fountain has the safest water?	Location (amount of use)	Bacteria in the water	• Source of water to the drinking fountains • Can dogs reach the drinking fountain? (yukky, but realistic) • Exposure of fountains to outdoor environment
3. How do different drinks affect teeth?	Kinds of liquids	Condition of tooth enamel	• Number of times each drink is consumed in a day, and when • When and how often the person brushes their teeth • Other food that is eaten • Smoking • Heredity: what is the general health of each subject's parents' teeth?
4. Which laundry detergent cleans best?	Brand of detergent	Cleanliness of clothes washed	• Kind of dirt on the clothes • Length of time the clothes have been dirty • Wash water temperature • Amount of time clothes are washed

Got your Thinking Cap on? Good. Now it's time to figure out variables for your project. Start with the manipulated and responding variables, from your hypothesis. Then think of other variables that could affect the responding variable. Write everything in this table or make one like it in your project journal.

Project/Question	Manipulated variable (Input)	Responding Variable (Outcome)	Other variables that could affect the responding variable
			• • • • • •

Next you'll need to figure out how to control for those "other" variables. Below is an example using Nick's projec. This time, one variable per box is listed down the left column. Then the potential changes for each variable are identified, followed by ideas for how to control those changes.

Variable	What could be different	How it could be controlled
Manipulated variable: kind of bat material	Aluminum bat Wooden bat	Have each person hit 10 balls, switching back and forth between bats on each hit
Kind of ball	Hardball, softball, or whiffle ball (just kidding)	Use relatively new hardballs
Weather	Calm, windy, hot, cold, rainy, sunny	Choose a calm day. Record weather conditions at time of the test, just in case it becomes noteworthy later.
Batters	Could be males or females of any age or athletic ability	Since Nick is most concerned about which bat to use for Little League, he could select a few good batters from his team.
How ball is pitched	Depends on who's pitching: could be thrown fast, lobbed slowly, straight or curved	Have each batter just toss up the baseballs to themselves.

Now identify controls for *your* project:

Variable	What could be different	How it could be controlled
Manipulated variable:		

Science fair tip. Judges love to see creative ways to control those other variables or measure the responding variable. For example, one student made a kicking machine out of wood and an old shoe so soccer balls would be hit with the same force every time.

☞ Amy R. made a special device to quantify the measure of banana freshness. Her mother knew about tenderometers used in actual food labs. She helped Amy make one for her project using a small scale and toothpicks. You can see a picture of it in Chapter 7.

Here's a tip. If you want, you can practice controlling your variables before you start your actual project to see if your ideas actually work. You know, that ol' "ounce of prevention is worth a pound of trouble" idea.

After you have identified all your variables and how you'll control them, you're ready to develop your step-by-step procedures.

Important checkpoint.

If you're sure about the following items, then you're ready to design your procedures. Otherwise you might want to work on them some more before going to Step 3b.

    a. Your topic
    b. Your hypothesis
    c. Your manipulated and responding variables
    d. Other variables that could affect the outcome and how to control them

Step 3b: Develop your plan

This section will help you design your plan (called procedures by scientists). You must design your procedures and get approval before you start the experiment.

– IMPORTANT –

YOUR TEACHER MUST APPROVE YOUR PROCEDURES BEFORE YOU START THE ACTUAL EXPERIMENT! You may need other approvals, too, if you'll be using hazardous materials, human subjects or tissue, or vertebrate animals. The approval process is covered in Step 3d.

Your procedures should give clear directions that anyone could follow. They should tell what materials and equipment will be needed, how to start, and what to do step by step. They work a lot like a cook-book recipe.

Science Fair Note: You may have hopes of going on to science fairs at the regional or higher levels. If so, make sure you find out from your teacher which rules will apply. Look over the rules before you design your experiment. You may need to plan certain things into your procedures. For example, the Discovery Channel Young Scientist Challenge (DCYSC) requires a single picture of some aspect of your project. The picture cannot include you in it, and it cannot be a picture of your final display. It would be wise to plan for that picture as you develop your procedures.

Take a look at how Nick might have written his procedures, then use the Designing-your-procedures HELPER on page 26 for your own project.

1. Prior to the day of the test, get the coach's permission to use the football field for this experiment.
2. Pick a morning when the three subjects (Dad, brother, and I) can go to the school together. Choose a day with a forecast of calm wind and no rain.
3. Take materials on materials list.
4. Use the school's football field with yardage stripes for the test.

5. I'll stand at one goal line and hit 28 balls,[3] one at a time, alternating each hit between the wood and aluminum bats. (Batters toss each ball up to themselves and hit it; balls are not pitched.)

6. Have Dad spot where each ball lands and write the distance in the data table, using yardage markers to judge the distance.

7. After I'm finished, gather the baseballs and repeat steps 5 through 7, first with brother hitting, then Dad.

8. When we're finished, collect materials and go home.

Materials list:

    i. One aluminum bat (Copperhead CU31, 29 inches long)

    ii. One wood bat (Louisville Slugger 180-Jeff Bagwell Edition, 33 inches long).

    iii. Twenty-eight baseballs (my Dad's a Little League coach)

    iv. One football field with yardage markers (!)

    v. Data table, clipboard, and pencil

    vi. A long measuring tape

Note that Nick's procedures are complete and clear. Someone else could follow them and do the same exact experiment. In fact, Nick could repeat it two or three times using different batters in each test. Scientists often repeat experiments like that to be more sure of their results.

Remember this while you are planning your procedures: plan how you'll keep track of your data (measurements) and observations. Your data is a crucial element of your whole experiment. Thus it's important to organize it right from the start. You want your data to be complete and accurate.

Example: Nick needed a way to keep track of each batter's distances with each bat. He also knew he'd want to average the results later. Below is a table that would help him keep his data straight. Each box will show the distance for each hit.

Hit #	Nick		Pat		Dad	
	Alum.	Wood	Alum.	Wood	Alum.	Wood
1						
2						
3						
4						
5						
6						
7						
8						
9						
10						
11						
12						
13						
14						

---

3. Not everyone has 28 baseballs! Nick's Dad is a Little League coach. If he had fewer baseballs, he could modify his procedures accordingly.

Now use the Designing-your-procedures HELPER to develop your own plan.

Note: Make sure your procedures address these four questions:

1. How will the experiment begin? (What materials and equipment will you need, and how should they be set up?)
2. What changes will you make to the *manipulated* variable? (What will you change, how much will you change it, and how often?)
3. How will you measure the *responding* variable, and how often?
4. How will you *control* for the other variables?

As you develop your procedures, keep in mind what kind of equipment and materials you'll need. If you're not sure you can get or make them, find out before completing your plan. You may need to try a different approach.

DESIGNING-YOUR-PROCEDURES HELPER

1. Write your hypothesis here: _____

_____

2. List your manipulated variable: _____

3. What changes will occur in the manipulated variable? _____

_____

4. List your responding variable (outcome): _____

_____

5. What changes do you expect to see in you responding variable, and how will you measure those changes? (Example: With Nick it was distance the baseball traveled in the air.) _____

_____

_____

_____

Science fair tip: Sometimes it is difficult to get accurate measurements, like if something's hard to get to or it moves too fast. Judges love to see creative ways of overcoming these challenges.

6. How often should you measure changes in your responding variable? From your background information you should be able to figure out the time interval you'll need between measurements. (If you're tracking things like plant growth or banana freshness, you will need to take measurements every day or two. Other things, like baseball distance, may just need a one-time measurement.) _____

_____

_____

7. What units will you use when you measure? (All science projects should use metric units, e.g., grams, liters, meters. But if your measuring devices are in U.S., e.g., pounds, quarts, feet, no problem. Just access any of the numerous conversion sites on the Internet, such as http://www.onlineconversion.com/.) _____

_____

_____

8. List your *manipulated* variable: _____

_____

_____

9. How will you be changing your manipulated variable? (Examples: Nick had his batters alternate bats with each hit. Amy's manipulated variables were air temperature and amount of air for banana storage. She changed the temperature by putting some bananas in the refrigerator. She changed the amount of air by putting some in sealed zip-loc bags.) Describe how you'll change your manipulated variable: _____

_____

_____

_____

10. In the table on page 23 you wrote ideas on how to control all the other variables. Using those ideas and your answers above, write a short overview of how you might set up your whole experiment. Since this description will be longer than your other answers, write it in your journal. Then review it with your parent or teacher.

11. Would photographs be helpful during your experiment? Here are ways they can help:

 a. To show the set-up. When it comes time to make your display, you know the saying: "A picture is worth a thousand words."
 b. To show changes more easily through pictures than words. If you're not sure if photos would be helpful, take them anyway. It's much easier to go ahead and take them than to wish later that you had.

12. If you choose to use photos, here are some tips:

 a. Use a digital camera if you have access to one. Most digitals can zoom (close-up), plus you can tell right away if the picture suits your purposes or not.
 b. Include a recipe-size card in one corner of each photo. Write the date and time on it. This will make it easier to keep the pictures in order later.
 c. If size of objects is important, include a ruler in the picture.

13. You have thought through all these questions. Now write your step by step procedures. Again, it's probably best to do this in your journal.

14. **IMPORTANT:** Remember to get the approvals you need – *in writing and dated* – before you start your experiment. You'll need your teacher's approval for sure, and you may need additional approvals if you plan to use hazardous materials, vertebrate animals, or people in any way.

Step 3c – List and obtain your materials and equipment

 This step is simple. Go down your procedures and make a list of all the things you'll need to conduct your experiment. Remember the things you'll need for measuring, too.
 Here's a tip: Put a sticky note beside any step that requires materials or equipment. Write what you'll need to do that step on the sticky. When you're finished, put all the sticky notes on a piece of paper and copy the list into your journal.
 Don't give up right away if you find you need special equipment. Maybe your school or a local college or business would loan it to you. Or, maybe your family or teacher knows of someone who could help you make it. That's what Amy did for her banana tenderometer.
 Larger cities have scientific supply stores that sell special supplies for science projects. Chapter 9 includes contact information for Edmund Scientific. It is one of the country's largest scientific supply stores.

Step 3d – Get approval

 Your teacher should provide you with the approval forms used for your school's science fair. Many schools use the approval forms published by the International Science and Engineering Fair (ISEF). See Appendix B for information on these forms.
 YOU MUST GET APPROVAL BEFORE PROCEEDING with your experiment to ensure your research plan is safe to follow – for you, your subjects, and innocent bystanders! This is especially true if you'll be using hazardous materials or if you'll be using live subjects such as animals or people. And especially if 'people' means your little brother!

CHAPTER SUMMARY

Step 3: Develop your procedures	
Purpose of this step	Plan step-by-step procedures for your experiment so you can follow it just like a cookbook recipe.
Sub-steps	a. Identify variables and controls b. Develop your procedures c. List and obtain materials and equipment d. Get proper approval
Tips	• Be sure that any changes in your responding variable (outcome) can only be the result of your manipulated variable. Control for your other variables. • Plan how you will change the manipulated variable, and how often. • Estimate the time you'll need for each step. • Know in advance how you will measure your results. • Make a time-phased table or chart to record your data.
Tools	Designing-your-procedures HELPER
Traps	• Waiting 'til the last minute to develop your plan. • *Not* planning. This is the biggest mistake you could make.

Chapter 4

Step 4: Carry out your plan

Chapter preview	
Sub-steps:	a. Get out your procedures b. Follow them!
What happens in this step:	You'll follow the step-by-step procedures you developed in the last chapter. Record your observations and measurements according to your plan. Write your data in section 2 of your journal or on special forms like Nick's data table in the last chapter.
Time to allow:	Depends on your plan. You can estimate the time for each step and add it up.

Step 4 is easy:

a. Get out your procedures

b. Follow 'em!

Well, not quite *that* easy! Keep these things in mind as you follow your procedures and collect your data:

a. First, follow your procedures *exactly*. Measure accurately, and take the measurements at the interval you planned.

b. It's a good idea to jot down observations daily in your journal. Write down what you see along with the date and time. *Observations* means details about expected changes as well as unplanned events or problems you experience. Scientists never know which information will prove to be significant when all the data is analyzed. Keep accurate notes. These notes will be useful when it's time to analyze your data and draw conclusions.

☞   Many scientific advances have been made on data that at first seemed out of place. Penicillin, for example, was discovered in 1928 during an experiment with molds. It was noticed that certain molds dissolved common germs. One of those molds was used to develop one of the most important medicines in history – penicillin.

☞ Here's another reason that notes are important. In 1920, the heirs of a man named John Montgomery sued the U.S. Government for purchasing airplanes made by the Wright brothers. They claimed that Mr. Montgomery owned a patent on the airplanes, not the Wright brothers. Orville Wright's written deposition was packed with notes from research he and his brother conducted from 1899 to 1903, proving that they were in fact the inventors of all elements of their airplanes.

☞ Archimedes was one of the first to use applied mathematics, and he founded the science of mechanics – what we now call physics. But he was also an inventor of gadgets. Unfortunately, he was born into the Greek aristocracy in 287 B.C., where "gentlemen" were not supposed to tinker with mechanical things. Thus, even though Archimedes couldn't keep himself away from these devices, he was ashamed to keep notes on his achievements. We only know about them from tales handed down by others.

c. What if you get part way through your experiment and realize it's not going to work out? If you suspect your project is turning into a disaster, discuss it with your teacher or sponsor before you abandon or change it. If you change your procedures midstream, it usually means you'll have to begin your data collecting all over, and that will mean you need more time. Sometimes projects just don't work out, even with the best planning. Don't despair – there is still something to learn and you can report on that.

We learn more by looking for the answer to a question and not finding it than we do from learning the answer itself.
– Lloyd Alexander

CHAPTER SUMMARY

Purpose of this step	Carry out your plan
Sub-steps	a. Get out your procedures b. Follow 'em!
Tips	• Be objective • Take accurate measurements, at the right time • Be on the lookout for unexpected changes
Tools	Your procedures, materials and equipment
Traps	Having to stop and start over if you didn't plan your procedures carefully enough

Chapter 5

Interpret your results

The most exciting phrase to hear in science, the one that heralds the most discoveries, is not, "Eureka!" (I found it!) but "That's funny..."

— Isaac Asimov

Chapter preview	
Sub-steps:	5a – Analyze your data 5b – Draw conclusions
What happens in this step:	In this step you decide if your data supports your hypothesis or not. Either way, it's new knowledge. What's important here is that you make valid conclusions from your data, not that your original educated guess turned out to be correct.
Time to allow:	Two days to one week.

Step 5a – Analyze your data (determine what it means)

The data you collected in Step 4 is called "raw" data. You took several individual measurements and wrote them down, one by one. It is often hard to interpret data in its "raw" form. We'll use Nick's completed data table, below, as an example throughout this chapter. Recall that he measured the distance of hits using yard markers on the football field, so he initially wrote them down in yards. Science projects must always use metric units, so in the next step we'll show the distances converted to meters. Here is Nick's "raw" data:

	Nick		Pat		Dad	
(All distances initially measured in yards and will be converted to metric later)						
Hit #	Alum.	Wood	Alum.	Wood	Alum.	Wood
1	61	64	67	72	8	86
2	33	58	49	67	77	67
3	69	21	59	56	62	85
4	69	48	90	62	69	71
5	71	74	47	27	88	67
6	65	63	68	65	94	77
7	73	59	74	51	93	51
8	48	51	64	68	50	83
9	39	56	22	74	63	84
10	51	67	51	78	69	82
11	83	53	73	64	47	37
12	79	59	71	72	62	86
13	60	58	30	81	84	83
14	53	57	70	71	42	86

Tables

Tables are simply numbers or observations organized in columns. Tables are a convenient way to list specific measurements or observations, but they can be difficult to interpret, just like Nick's table, above.

What could Nick do with his data table to make it easier to analyze?

Averages

One thing Nick could do is summarize the individual distances using averages. Here's his table again. First he converted yards to meters (metric). He found that 1 yard = 0.914 meter. He then multiplied each distance in yards by 0.914. Then he added a row to the table where he put the average distance of each column :

	Nick		Pat		Dad	
	(All distances have been converted to meters)					
Hit #	Alum.	Wood	Alum.	Wood	Alum.	Wood
1	55.7	58.5	53.9	65.8	75.9	78.6
2	30.2	53.0	44.8	53.9	70.4	53.9
3	63.1	19.2	53.9	51.2	56.7	77.7
4	63.1	66.7	82.3	56.7	63.1	64.9
5	64.9	67.6	43.0	24.7	80.4	61.2
6	59.4	57.6	46.6	59.4	85.9	70.4
7	66.7	53.9	46.6	46.6	85.0	46.6
8	43.9	46.6	46.6	46.6	45.7	75.9
9	35.6	51.2	20.1	46.6	46.6	70.4
10	46.6	61.2	46.6	73.2	63.1	71.9
11	75.9	46.6	66.7	58.5	43.0	33.8
12	72.2	53.9	64.9	65.8	56.7	78.6
13	54.8	46.6	27.4	74.0	76.8	46.6
14	48.4	52.1	64.0	64.9	38.4	78.6
Average	55.75	52.48	50.53	56.28	63.41	65.15

This is a little better, but still not totally clear. Nick wondered if an overall average for each type of bat would be helpful. He took the averages for each bat, and averaged them. He added another section for these averages in the lower left corner of his table:

14	48.4	52.1	64.0	64.9	38.4	78.6
Average	55.75	52.48	50.53	56.28	63.41	65.15
	Alum.	Wood				
Overall Average	56.56	57.97				

At this point, Nick could conclude that the wood bat hits the farthest. But he still wanted a better way of seeing how each batter did with each bat. He decided to try a bar chart.

---

4. To average each column, add all the distances and divide by the total number of hits (14).

Bar Chart

A bar chart[5] gave Nick a more visual comparison of the batters. He decided to include the overall average, too. He still concluded that the wood bat gave the overall best results. He also noted that the bar chart would look good when it came time to make his display.

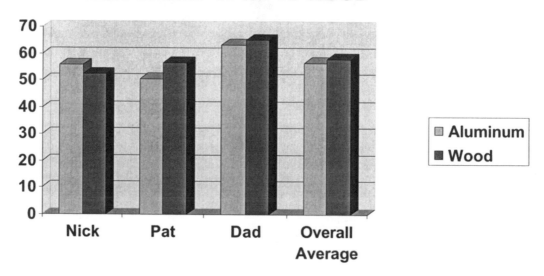

There is one final way Nick could analyze his results. If one person had consistently hit very long or very short they would offset (skew) the average. What else could Nick do? He could count up how many batters hit farther with one bat than another. Here's what that would look like:

Batter	Aluminum	Wood
Nick	√	
Pat		√
Dad		√
Total number who hit farthest with each bat:	1	2

Notice that Nick placed a check mark under the type of bat each person hit farthest with, and then totaled the number of people who hit farthest with each bat. This technique would be more helpful with a larger number of batters, but at least you can see how it works.

---

5. For a more complete description on using charts and graphs, see the section titled "Additional Information about Analyzing Results" later in this chapter.

5b – Draw conclusions

So what would you conclude from Nick's results? Here is his hypothesis; would you accept it or reject it?

If college baseball players' batting averages and home runs declined when they could only use wood bats, then I think my family will hit farther with aluminum than with wood bats.

Nick had to reject his hypothesis. Although *he* hit farther with the aluminum bat, his brother and Dad hit farther with wood.

Let's look at that word *reject*. Remember what you learned back in step 2? Your hypothesis is an educated guess. It doesn't matter if it turns out to be correct or not. It merely helps you define your variables and design your procedures. If your hypothesis turns out to be correct, scientists say it is *supported*. If your results don't support the hypothesis, they say it is *rejected*. Used in this sense, it is purely a factual term, not meant to be judgmental. Either way – whether your hypothesis turns out to be correct or not – you learn something new, and that's the whole idea.

What scientists *don't* say, if the hypothesis is supported, is that they *proved* something to be true. In fact, there are scientists who say the only way we know something for sure about a hypothesis is to disprove it.[6] Every hypothesis that is supported has a chance of later being shown to be false, when we learn more about it.

☞   Aristotle lived around 350 B.C. He had many ideas which shaped the field of science. He thought that different sets of natural laws governed the movement of objects on earth and in space. In the early 1600's Sir Isaac Newton figured out that whether it was apples or moons, objects obeyed the same three laws of motion. Aristotle's hypothesis seemed "true" for 2,000 years. Then Newton disproved it.

The greatest obstacle to discovering the shape of the earth, the continents, and the ocean was not ignorance but the illusion of knowledge.
— Daniel J. Boorstin, *The Discoverers*

Drawing conclusions – part 2

Earlier you saw how Nick arrived at his conclusion. Let's take a closer look at these little creatures called conclusions. They require special care and feeding. Judges will want to know why you reached the conclusion you did. They may also want to know what else you're thinking now that you have your conclusion. Like: "Would you change anything if you were to do your experiment again?" Or: "What other questions do your results raise that you or someone else could explore?"

---

6. See Platt, "Strong Inference," in the bibliography.

Here are the things your conclusion should address, using examples from Nick's experiment:

1. Your conclusion must match your data *and* answer your hypothesis.

There are two parts to this item.

a. Two of Nick's three batters hit farthest with the wooden bat. He might be tempted to conclude that two thirds of all batters would have the same result. But he used a pretty small sample: himself, his brother and his Dad. Therefore, his conclusion really only applies to his family. If he wanted to learn which bat most guys on his Little League team hit farthest with, how should he change his experiment?

b. You might learn several things from your data. This could lead to more than one conclusion. Make sure one of them answers your hypothesis! Don't let yourself get side-tracked and forget about your original question. The main question to answer is whether your results support or reject your hypothesis.

2. If you ended up rejecting your hypothesis, can you offer a reason or two why that might have happened? For example, did your data not support your hypothesis? Was your conclusion different from that proposed by your hypothesis?

People learn something every day, and a lot of times it's that what they learned the day before was wrong.
– Bill Vaughan

Nick was surprised by his results. His background information revealed that metal bats have been banned in college baseball because too many batters were hitting it out of the ball park. After metal bats were banned, batting averages and the number of homeruns declined. So why did Nick get different results?

The first thing to check is the data itself. Is it accurate? Nick knew his distance measures were correct – he and his Dad had double checked each ball as it landed. He rechecked his procedures, examined his bats, and... Oh-oh. The wood bat was four inches longer and a few ounces heavier than the metal bat. That could explain why his Dad and brother hit farther with it. It might also explain why Nick was the one who hit farther with the metal bat: he's the smallest of the three people and probably couldn't swing the heavier bat as fast. Case closed.

None of this is bad news. Nick learned something. He has an explanation for his unexpected results. And he has some ideas for follow-on research, should he or someone else want to pursue it.

Consider these questions when explaining your results:

1. **How precise were your measurements?** If you use a standard ruler, you can measure to the nearest 1/16th of an inch, or to one millimeter. Nick used the yardage markings on a football field. To what level of precision were his measures? He didn't need 16ths of an inch; he only needed yards. So that's how he recorded his data, to the nearest yard. There is no right or wrong level of precision; it just needs to match the nature of the change you'll be measuring.

2. **Did your measuring device measure what you intended?** With Nick's project, the answer is yes. He needed to measure distance, and he did. Look at Amy's banana freshness project in Chapter 7. How did she measure freshness?

3. **How reliable do you think your results are?** That is, if someone were to repeat your experiment using the exact same procedures, do you think they would get the same results? Can you now see some uncontrolled variables at play? If so, how did they affect your results? Could you figure out a better way to control for them next time?

4. **How valid do you think your results are?** Chances are that your experiment didn't duplicate the real world exactly. How did those differences affect the way your conclusion applies to the real situation? For example, Nick had his subjects toss the ball up to themselves. But in a real game the ball would be pitched. Could this difference affect hitting distances? You don't have to go repeat your experiment if you now recognize a factor like this; just be able to discuss how it might affect the validity of your results.

5. **How does your sample size and number of trials affect your conclusion?** Here's a rule of thumb: a large random sample is normally better than a small hand-picked sample. And more trials are always better than a few. Larger samples and more trials help to verify your results. What could Nick do to draw a correct conclusion about his whole team?

6. **What ideas can you suggest for further research?** This is an important question. Scientists never feel like they have the final answer. One piece of new knowledge usually raises more questions, and if you can suggest one or two from your research, good on ya!

Additional information about analyzing results

This section gives a more complete description of ways to analyze data. It covers graphs, charts, and basic math like averages and medians. This material is only for reference. If you don't need it, skip to the chapter summary on page 40.

Graphs and charts

Graphs and charts can often compress data into a more manageable format. Three types are commonly used in science projects. Each type is best used for a specific purpose.

Pie charts are used to show proportions of a whole. For example, say you wanted to depict the percentage of fat contained in various types of meat. A separate pie chart for each type of meat would be very effective. A wedge in each pie would visually show what proportion of that meat is made up by fat.

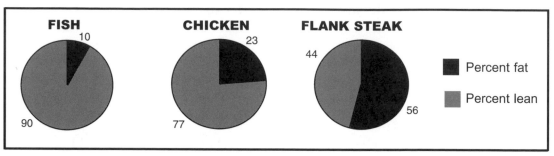

Pie Charts (Steak and Chicken): *Physician's Committee for Responsible Medicine*, Spring / Summer 2000, Vol. IX, No. 2, downloaded from http://perm.org/magazine/GM00SpringSummer /GM00SpSum2.html on June 9, 2005. Pie Chart (Fish): New York Seafood Council, downloaded from http://www.nyseafood.org/nutrition/health2.asp on June 9, 2005.

Bar charts are used to show comparisons. That's the kind of chart Nick used on page 34.

Line graphs are used to show trends over time. For example, a line graph would be very effective to show the growth (height) of plants over a period of sevveral days, like this:

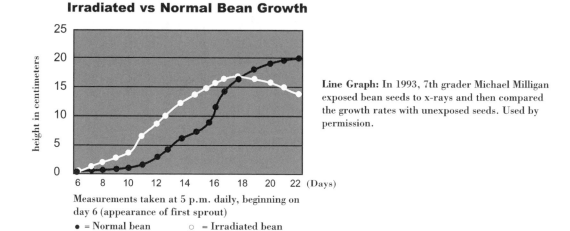

Line Graph: In 1993, 7th grader Michael Milligan exposed bean seeds to x-rays and then compared the growth rates with unexposed seeds. Used by permission.

When should you use a bar chart vs. a line graph? Follow these guidelines:

a. Line graphs are best used for things that change over time and are continuous. If you're plotting plant growth, it's the same plant from one day to the next, and its height one day is related to how high it was the day before. Thus a line graph gives a visual picture of the plant's growth over time.

b. Bar charts are best used for things that are not continuous. With Nick's baseball distances, each hit is a new one. Hit #2 doesn't depend on how far hit #1 was. It wouldn't make any sense to connect the distances for each hit, so Nick chose a bar chart showing length of average hit. In Amy's case where each banana got riper every day (in some cases, real ripe!), a line graph was the best choice. See her graph on p. 53.

No matter what type of graph or chart is used, it should show the data clearly. Titles and labels should be easy to understand. Time or the manipulated variable is usually placed along the bottom, or X, axis. The responding variable is placed along the vertical, or Y, axis. Choose ranges of values for the axes that cover all the data.

Means and medians (simple math)

You already saw averages in Nick's experiment. Nick was able to use a single value – the average – to represent all 14 hits for each bat by each batter.

Mean. What we generally think of as an average is called the *mean*, in math terms. It is a very common way to represent a whole group with one number, like Nick did. The mean is calculated by adding up all the values, then dividing by the number of measurements taken. If we wanted to know the mean height of five students, we would calculate it like this:

Student	Height (in cm)	
1	142	
2	160	
3	135	
4	151	
5	122	
Total: 5	710	Mean = 710/5 = 142 cm (about 4'8")

Median - The median is the center value in a range of measurements. It represents a group better than the mean when there are big differences at either end of the range. This is why they use the median, rather than the mean, to depict such values as wage-earners' income or home values. (A few very rich folks would make the mean too large to represent the group as a whole.) Here's how you calculate the median. Using the height of our group of classmates, we would first rearrange the data in order of increasing height, like this:

Student	Height (in cm)
5	122
3	135
1	**142**
4	151
2	160

The median is defined as the middle value in the list. In this case the mean is 142 cm. If there were an even number of values, we would take the average of the two in the middle.

How a computer can help with data analysis

Most computers come with spreadsheet programs that can automatically calculate things like totals and means. These programs can also be used to create tables, graphs, or charts. Even word processing programs let you create tables with simple calculations. If you don't know how to use these features, ask someone to show you.

CHAPTER SUMARY

Step 5 - Interpret your results	
Purpose of this step	In this step you decide if your data supports your hypothesis or not. Either way, it's new knowledge. What's important is that you make valid conclusions from your data about your hypothesis. It is okay if your data doesn't support your original educated guess.
Sub-steps	5a – Analyze your data 5b – Draw conclusions
Tips	• Use tables, graphs, and charts to help analyze your data. • Also use simple math like averages (means) and medians. • Make sure your conclusion matches your data. • Be able to explain your results and your conclusion. • Describe what you'd do differently based on what you know now. • Suggest questions that could be explored next.
Tools	• Computer spreadsheets
Traps	• Getting side-tracked and drawing a conclusion that doesn't answer the hypothesis. • Getting caught up in thinking your hypothesis had to be correct. • Extending your conclusion to a broader range of subjects than your data represent.

Chapter 6

It's what you learn after you know it all that counts.
— John Wooden

Step 6: Communicate your results

Chapter preview	
Sub-steps:	a. Write your research report b. Make your display c. Present your project verbally

What happens in this step:	Science is about learning. Remember the three main questions scientists seek to answer?
	    1. What is it?
	    2. How does it work?
	    3. Why does it work that way?
	You'll describe your question, how you set about answering it, and what you learned in the end, both expected and unexpected. The three sub-steps listed above each serve a slightly different purpose:
	a. Report: detailed report of all the work you did.
	b. Display: Eye-catching summary of main elements.
	c. Verbal Presentation: Gives you a chance to share what you have learned with others.

Time to allow:	One week – or more.

Introduction to this chapter

Science is all about learning – and then sharing what we learn so others can explore new questions. Scientists share what they learn at conferences, in books and articles, and every time two or more of them meet.

For you, "sharing" translates into "science fair." Just like your project up to this point, you just need to understand the process. That's what this chapter is about. By knowing the science fair process and what to expect, you should not only breeze through it, but enjoy the journey, too!

Science fairs enable you to share your project with others in three ways, so here's how this chapter is organized:

    a. Written report
    b. Visual display
    c. Brief verbal presentation and question-and-answer session

Step 6a - Write your research report

The research report is a clear written summary of your whole project. Find out from your teacher what format your school follows. Regardless of the final format, the Research Report HELPER in this section will help you organize the key elements to include in your report.

Your final report should be typed (or printed from the computer), double spaced, with one-inch margins on top, bottom, and both sides. Use font size 12. One page like that contains about 250 words.

RESEARCH REPORT HELPER[7]

Suggestion: Use the third section of your project journal to jot answers to these questions. If you kept notes along the way then your answers are already in your notes – all you're doing here is organizing the key points.

1. Your report should give someone who is not closely involved with your project a clear picture of your question or hypothesis, how you went about solving it, and what you concluded. In no more than two pages,[8] address the following questions:

a. How did you get your idea?

b. Who else helped you with your project? Describe the kind of help they gave you.

c. Who supervised your work? (This may already be answered by 'a' and 'b' above.)

d. What was your hypothesis or question?

e. Give an overview of your experimental procedures. What was your general strategy for setting up the experiment and collecting data?

f. Be sure to describe any special challenges you faced and how you dealt with them. For example, did you have to make a unique device either for setting up the experiment or measuring the data?

g. Was your hypothesis supported or rejected? Why?

h. If you did your experiment as a team with one or two other students, here are some additional questions to answer in no more than about 2/3 of a page:

i. What role did each team member play (i.e., planning, conducting, and presenting the project)?

ii. Why was the project better by having more than one person work on it?

---

7. The questions in this HELPER correspond to the questions in Part III of DCYSC's entry forms.
8. DCYSC allows 500 words for this question, which is about two typed pages, double spaced.

2. What one visual image best shows the nature of your project? Example: For Nick's project, his bar chart (on page 34) conveys in a single "picture" how he set up his experiment (three batters, two types of bats) and what his results were. This visual aid must meet these requirements:

    a. It can be a picture, diagram, table, chart, or graph.

    b. It must fit on one 8.5" x 11" piece of paper (or the DCYSC entry form, which has slightly less space).

    c. If it's a picture, you cannot appear in it.

    d. It cannot be audio, video or text other than captions or the actual data like the numbers in Nick's data table.

3. In no more than one typed, double spaced page,[9] reflect on your overall results.

    a. What are one or two key things you learned from your project?

    b. Did anything surprise you along the way? How did you deal with it?

    c. If you could do this experiment over, would you do anything differently to make it better? What and why?

    d. Did your results raise any new questions that could be explored?

> ***Science ... never solves a problem without creating ten more.***
> **– George Bernard Shaw**

4. Now we take a slightly different slant. Remember when you were asked why your project could be of interest to others? This is an "ah-ha!" question. It examines whether your project is just a casual, "fill a square" effort, or whether it really contributes valuable knowledge. Choose either 'a' or 'b' below ... you're not expected to do both. There is a 500 word limit (about two double-spaced typed pages).

a. Write an article for your local newspaper that explains what significance or importance your project has for the community. What impact does your project have on them, or why should they care about your results?

b. Or, if you have actually communicated your project to others – not counting your science fair presentation – describe what you did and what the reaction was.

---
9. A maximum of 250 words.

Your teacher or school may require you to use the DCYSC entry forms. If so, your answers to the Research Report HELPER should be easy to plug into these forms. You'll also need your data tables and analysis results. Here is another common format that some schools use if they do not the official DCYSC forms:

1. **Title page.** Title of project, your name and your teacher's name, and date.

2. **Abstract page.** One page overview of project; should give the reader a good idea of what the project is about and what the important results were.

3. **Table of Contents.** List all sections and the page number on which each one starts.

4. **Introduction.** Describe why you chose this topic, provide the background information you gathered, and state your hypothesis. Briefly explain why you feel this topic is important.

5. **Methods.** Describe your procedures and include your list of materials.

6. **Results.**

   a. List all the data you gathered during the project. Include your journal as part of the exhibit. Judges like to see that students gathered data carefully and at regular intervals.

   b. Show how you analyzed your data, including tables, graphs, and statistics.

   c. Describe what happened. Results should only describe *what you actually observed*. Results should *not* describe *why* you think something happened – that goes in the conclusion.

7. **Conclusion.** State whether your hypothesis was supported or rejected. Describe why you believe the result happened, based on your research. Based on what you learned from this project, how could your information be helpful to someone else?

8. **Acknowledgements.** List any people who helped you in person, such as your teacher, parents, or perhaps an adult expert.

9. **Bibliography (references):** list the written sources you used for this project. Check science project rules for current format, or if none are given, use the format shown in Appendix E.

Step 6b - Make your display

The main feature of every school science fair is the displays. This is your chance to communicate your project visually. Anyone strolling by should be able to grasp what your project was about and what you learned. Normally displays go in a room like a science lab or the cafeteria. Step 6c describes what happens during judging.

For beginning projects, students often purchase 3-piece cardboard display boards made especially for science projects. They're roughly 4 feet wide by 2.5 feet tall. However, your display should be designed to suit the needs of your project.

Here are some diagrams of typical display boards, and two photographs of senior-level project displays that went to the International level of competition:

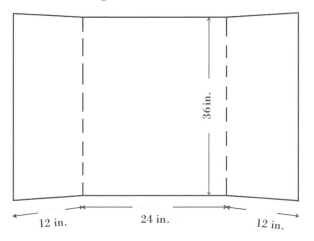

Above, Michael Milligan's 5-year project to develop a practical dielectic imaging system. Below Brigid Milligan's 4-year project, "The Effects of Electromagnetic Radiation on Polar and Nonpolar Molecular Uptake by K-12 Wild Type E Coli."

Above, a standard store-bought cardboard display. Below, display boards like those in the photographs. This is a fairly common design at higher level competitions.

DISPLAY BOARDS

At right, display boards made from .25 in. masonite and 1 x 2 in. wooden framing. The masonite's slick surface allows the display to be re-used for several years. The central panel and side wings are hinged, but with easily removed hinge pins. The table and shelf are held together with six wood screws. The entire display can be dismantled and boxed in a few minutes.

IMPORTANT:

Size restrictions vary among schools and school districts, and occasionally change even at the International level. *Be sure to check on the size rules before constructing an elaborate display!!*

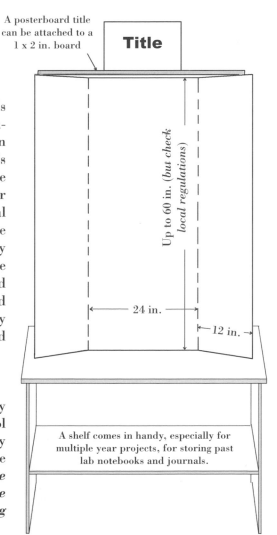

Your display should give a good summary of your project without looking cluttered. Here's what should be on it:

1. Title, usually centered at the top of the display. Does your choice of words create suspense (and invite the viewer to look closer)?

2. Purpose or question.

3. Statement of your hypothesis.

4. Procedure – how did you conduct the experiment? (Can be abbreviated.)

5. Show at least some of your data.

6. A photograph or drawing showing the setup.

7. Tables, charts or graphs showing your results.

8. Conclusion. Include a statement of whether your hypothesis was supported, and why or why not.

It's a good idea to sketch your display before you assemble it, to see how all the sections will be placed. It's much easier to change a sketch than re-make the real display!

Someone looking at the display should quickly see the main points. These features should be prominent: title, hypothesis, method, summary of data (use graphs or tables), and the conclusion. Use photographs to show key features of the project. You should place your full research report on the countertop with your display for anyone wanting to see more details.

Step 6c - Present your project verbally

You will normally be asked to discuss your project verbally for five to ten minutes with your teacher, class, or judges. Does that thought make you break out in a cold sweat? If so, you're not alone. This is an area that many students stress over. But there's a way to prevent that: preparation. Sure, you say.

Here, we'll show you. The faculty at Selah School District in Washington State has developed some clear and complete guidance on preparing for the verbal presentation. It is on the next page in the form of a Verbal Presentation HELPER:[10]

It will be important for you to be able to give a concise and confident summary of the project. You will be asked questions about your project and you want to be prepared to answer the questions in a very clear and thorough manner. Obviously, this requires that you really know your project! As part of your preparation, practice at home with family members, in front of a mirror, or video camera.

The first "real" oral presentation will be in front of your peers and teacher. Take the time to practice and prepare a handy set of notes (preferably on index cards). The notes should only be "main ideas." Don't read from the cards! Use the cards only if you lose concentration.

---

10. Brown, Mike, "How to present your science project."
http://www.selah.wednet.edu/JHS/Brown/howpresentproj.html#topofpresentpage
Downloaded Aug. 31, 2003. Used by permission.

VERBAL PRESENTATION HELPER [11]

1. Describe your project. Remember, you usually only have five to ten minutes for your entire presentation, so get right to the point on each of these items.

   a. State the title of the project.

   b. State why you are trying to solve that problem and why you think the project would benefit society.

   c. State the hypothesis.

   d. Quote a source to support the hypothesis. [12]

   e. Explain the experimental design:

      1) what variables were held constant?

      2) what was the manipulated variable? [13]

      3) how many variations of the manipulated variable did you have?

      4) what was the responding variable?

      5) what was measured and how was it measured? (In SI units [metric])

   f. Describe the materials.

   g. Explain the procedures (briefly, describing just the main points).

   h. Explain the results, referring to your graphs or tables.

   i. Discuss the conclusions and whether the results support the hypothesis.

   j. Describe new questions raised by the results.

   k. Make recommendations for someone who might want to try the experiment.

   l. Be prepared to answer questions from the audience.

2. Use good communication skills

   a. Use good posture, stand still, and maintain eye contact with the audience or judge.

   b. Communicate thoughts that are organized with a clear sequence of ideas.

   c. Use clear and effective delivery by varying tone, pitch and pace of speech.

   d. Use effective language, complete sentences and language well-suited to the audience and related to the science project. Avoid gesturing too much.

---

11. Ibid. Adapted by the author.
12. Note that Nick made his educated guess based on results from professional and college players. To really score points with the judges, it would be even better if he could discuss the science behind his choice. For example, what is it about bat material (wood vs. aluminum) that would explain why these players hit farther with aluminum?
13. Reminder: Some judges use the terms *independent* and *dependent* instead of *manipulated* and *responding*.

Here are some final tips that may help you feel confident and relaxed going into the verbal presentation.

1. First, realize that one source of nervousness is talking face-to-face with people you don't know. Remedy: treat the presentation more like a conversation than a speech. Take two or three slow, deep breaths just before it's your turn.

2. Be enthusiastic and proud of your work! You have put a lot of time and effort into this project. No one knows your project better than you do.

3. Judges enjoy seeing your project, your methods, and your conclusions. If they ask you questions, it's because they're interested in what you did.

4. If you don't know the answer to a question, say so, then don't worry about it. Judges don't expect you to know everything.

CHAPTER SUMMARY

Step 6 – Communicate your results	
Purpose of this step	Share what you learned from your research with others. And, compete for awards or scholarships if that's your goal, by advancing to regional or national level competitions.
Sub-steps	d. Write your research report e. Make your display f. Present your project verbally
Tips	• Be clear and concise in all three modes of communicating. • Focus on the key elements of your project
Tools	• Rules for the science fair you're entering, including your school and DCYSC or ISEF. • Computer programs for word processing, spreadsheets, graphics.
Traps	• Lack of preparation – not being able to tell the clear story about your project.

PART B: ADDITIONAL INFORMATION

Chapter 7

One student's project from start to finish

<u>What Kind of Conditions Do Bananas Like?</u>
By: Amy Robinson

BACKGROUND

<u>The Banana Plant</u>
    Bananas are fruit that are mistakenly thought to grow on trees. They, in fact, grow on a green, non-woody plant with a "trunk." Banana plants grow 10 to 25 feet tall. They grow in hot, damp climates. They succeed in rich, sandy soil that has good drainage. The workers pick the bananas when they are green so that when the bananas reach their destination, they will have ripened and appear yellow in stores. They also do this because bananas lose flavor the longer they are on the plant. Like most fruits it can be eaten raw or cooked.

A banana plant

<u>Bananas</u>
    People in the United States buy around 11 billion bananas. That is not very surprising because bananas are the most popular fruit in the United States. Bananas are about 0.5% fat, 1% protein, 23% carbohydrates, and 74% water.

<u>Tenderometer</u>
    Tenderometers can measure the tenderness of all sorts of fruit, vegetables, and especially wheat (such as spaghetti and other noodles) and meats. It is very important to know the tenderness of these two things because than you will know when they are finished cooking. People also use tenderometers for fruits to tell when they are ripe. Tenderometers are famous for measuring the tenderness of peas though. It measures these things by putting pressure on the object. They then measure how much pressure it took to puncture the object

Commercially available Tenderometer

PROBLEM

Storing bananas so that they stay at the perfect ripeness is always a problem. I decided to compare ways of keeping bananas. I want to see which is best.

HYPOTHESIS

I am doing this experiment to see which is the best method for keeping bananas I expect that the refrigerator bananas will be bad tasting and hard because the coldness might make the enzymes slow down and slow the ripening of the bananas.

I also expect that the bananas in Ziploc with air, Ziploc without air, and grocery store bags will be the softest because bags trap in heat. Heat may accelerate the ripening of bananas.

My hypothesis is that air and warmer temperatures speed up the ripening of bananas. If it is correct, I assume that the bananas out in the open will be perfect since they are at room temperature and have the most air of the five groups of bananas.

METHOD

Unripe (green) bananas will be divided into 5 groups of 3 bananas each.

#1. Refrigerator
#2. Ziploc, no air
#3. Ziploc, with air
#4. No container
#5. Store bag

On days 0, 2, 5 and 8 the bananas will be taste tested by two judges. They will also be tested for hardness using aa tenderometer that we will build ourselves. In the tenderometer, we will measure the amount of weight needed to puncture a banana with a skewer.

RESULTS

At the beginning (day 0) the bananas were very green and hard. We took one of the bananas and measured its weight, tenderness and skin thickness.

After one day all of the bananas were looking much riper except for the refrigerator bananas.

On the second day we tested the bananas the same way we did on the first day. We tested one banana out of each group. We also taste tested them. No one liked the refrigerator banana. One of the two judges like the second day bananas but the other one did not.

After five days, we did all of the tests on the bananas. Most of the bananas were too ripe, except for the refrigerator bananas. They were still not ripe enough.

CONCLUSION

After eight days the Ziploc without air bananas stayed in the Best Eating Range the longest, but the Ziploc with air bananas were about the same.

The store bag and the no container bananas ripened very quickly and were out of the Best Eating Range by the fifth day.

The refrigerator bananas were never in the Best Eating Range.

Knowing all of this information brings a conclusion that keeping bananas in Ziploc bag is the best way to keep bananas in the Best Eating Range the longest.

Another discovery of my experiment is that air speeds up the ripening of bananas.

BIBLIOGRAPHY

http://www.rbgkew.org.uk/ksheets/banana.htm

http://www.extento.hawaii.edu/kbase/crop/crops/i_banana.htm

http://www.foodtechcorp.com/tms2000.htm

Effect of Storage Conditions upon Banana Tenderness

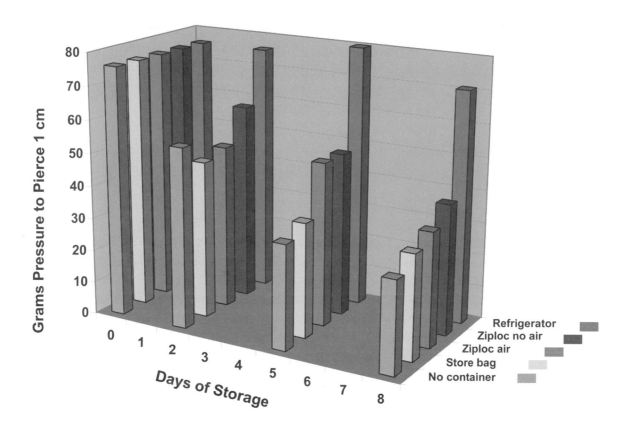

Effect of Storage Condtions upon Taste Testing Quality

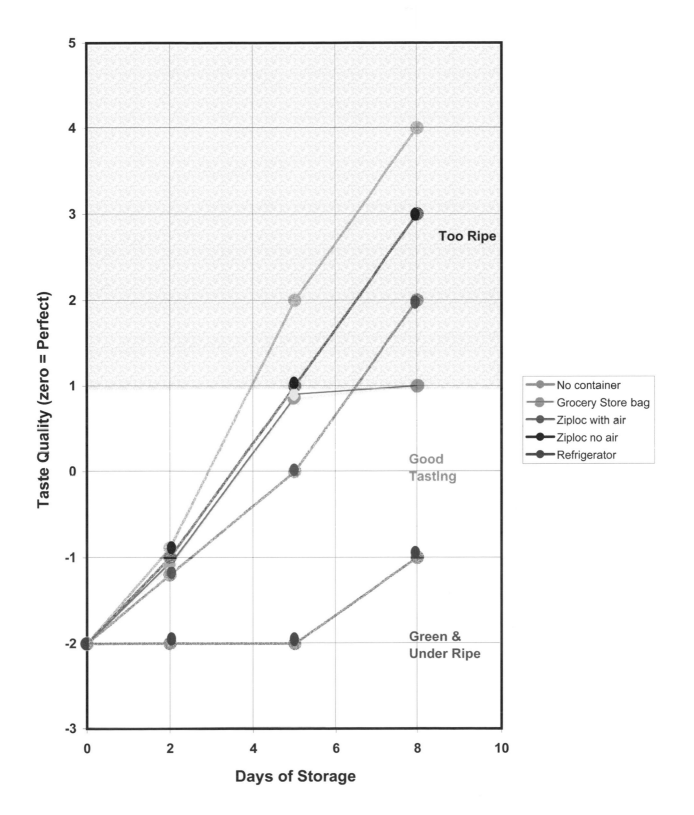

Taste
Testing Data

Days of Storage	Ripeness (Avg Score)				
	No container	Grocery Store bag	Ziploc with air	Ziploc no air	Refrigerator
0	-2	-2	-2	-2	-2
2	-1	-1	-1	-1	-2
5	2	1	0	1	-2
8	4	1	2	3	-1

Days of Storage	Ripeness Taster #1				
	No container	Grocery Store bag	Ziploc with air	Ziploc no air	Refrigerator
0	-2	-2	-2	-2	-2
2	0	0	0	0	-2
5	2	1	0	2	-2
8	4	1	2	4	-1

Days of Storage	Ripeness Taster #2				
	No container	Grocery Store bag	Ziploc with air	Ziploc no air	Refrigerator
0	-2	-2	-2	-2	-2
2	-2	-2	-2	-2	-2
5	2	1	0	0	-2
8	4	1	2	2	-1

Legend

-2 = Not Ripe: Too Green
-1 = Still Not Ripe: Somewhat Too Green
0 = Perfect Tasting Banana
1 = Somewhat too Ripe
2 = Much Too Ripe
4 = Over Ripe: Mushy and Brown

Weighing a Banana

Using the Tenderometer

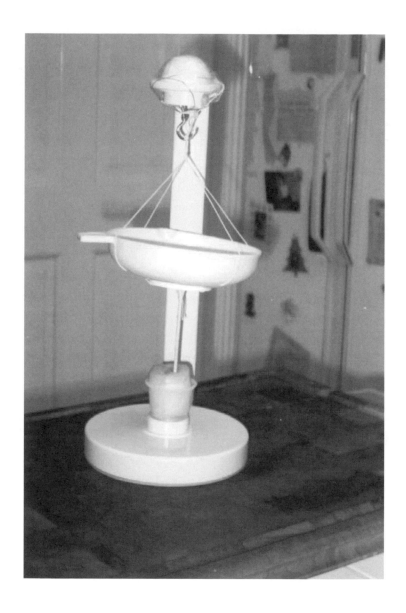

Measuring How Much Pressure It Takes to Puncture the Banana

Weighing the Pennies
That Were Used to Generate Pressure

Chapter 8

Tips for parents

Listening is a magnetic and strange thing, a creative force. The friends who listen to us are the ones we move toward. When we are listened to, it creates us, makes us unfold and expand.

– Karl Menninger

Parents, you have two very important roles: listen, and encourage.

The hardest and most important part of the whole science project is right at the beginning: picking the topic. And then, picking the specific question your child wants to explore. To your child, this can feel like entering a dark and winding tunnel. They can't see where they'll end up yet, and they haven't a clue what they'll encounter inside. What, you don't either? No problem! Your role is easy: listen, and encourage. That's all you have to do. (Of course, you can do more if you're familiar with the scientific method or your area of expertise happens to be the topic your child chose. You won't do the project *for* them, of course, but you can give a bit more technical assistance than some other parents, perhaps.)

Listen, and encourage. Oh – and in order to have something to listen to, ask. What do you ask? That's easy: the questions in the Topic HELPER (p.4). And the HELPER questions in whatever step your child is in.

To listen better, probe. Ask things like, "What is it about that topic that interests you? What kind of things have you been wondering about that topic? If you could know something more about it, what would it be?"

Here's a way to really impress your kid. When he or she is designing their procedures, walk up, look over their shoulder, and say, "Tell me the changes you expect to see in your manipulated variable." (To see what this means, read pp.19-26)

As the parent, you don't even have to write anything. Your child should have a project journal to write down their thoughts and answers. See, parents have it easy!

The second hardest part of a project isn't a step at all. It's to keep going. To your student, a science project probably seems like a daunting task. Heck, it may seem that way to you, too! For most kids, a science project is the longest-running assignment they've ever had. And every step of the way can seem like a new tunnel: dark, mysterious, no end in sight. But you know that it's like a lot of things in life. Break it down and do it one piece at a time. That's where part A of this book comes in.

Your role is to encourage your student (and not to get in the way!). Celebrate the completion of each major step (Chapters 1 through 6). Then huddle up and make plans for the next big play. Your child may have times when he wants to quit. Or do a mediocre job of planning. Or not check that her conclusion connects with her hypothesis (a too-frequent mistake with first-time project people, by the way). You don't have to do the rah-rah stuff all the time. But do stay attuned to their feelings and emotions. Listen beyond their words to the underlying meaning. Is he overwhelmed, feeling there's no end to this thing? Scared? Afraid her display won't be as sharp-looking as so-and-so's?

Listen and encourage. That's your role.

Here are a few other things you can do:

1. Make sure you and your student are using the current rules: this year's, and for the fair your school is affiliated with. Usually that'll be DCYSC for middle school and ISEF for senior high.

2. Know if the teacher has given your student a time table, and help them to remain on schedule.

3. Take them and their buddies to the library, the science fair, and anywhere else they need to go. To get swamp water maybe, or to visit your favorite scientific supply store.

4. Help your student find a good, safe, knowledgeable mentor. That might be you, a neighbor, a friend who is knowledgeable about your child's chosen topic, anyone whose expertise can help guide them through the process.

5. Your student will create a materials list. Even before that, they'll design their experiment. You can help them brainstorm slick substitutes for expensive equipment, or even just how to set up a simple schedule for measuring bean plants. Either way, help, encourage – but don't do it for 'em! (And don't get in the way!)

6. Help your student prepare for the oral presentation. You can guess how: listen to them practice, and encourage them. Ask them the questions on p. 47 that the judges may be asking them, so they can practice thinking on their feet.

7. Help your child to actually use the scientific method in their daily lives. (See Chapter 11.) When you hear her say something like, "So-and-so said…," ask how she knows that's true. Or how she could find out. If his answer includes words like hypothesis and variable, sit back and relax. Your kid isn't likely to get snookered by anyone!

Chapter 9

Resources for science projects

This chapter contains just a sampling of the hundreds of resources available to help with science projects in scientific supply houses, bookstores and on the internet.

Scientific equipment and supplies:

Edmund Scientific in Barrington, New Jersey (phone 1-609-457-8880)
Web address: http://scientificsonline.com/default.asp

Lasers and optical supply: MWK Industries, 1-800-356-7714.
Web address: http://mwklasers.com/index.htm

Science Project Advisor: an interactive CD-ROM to help guide students through a science project. Web address: http://shop.store.yahoo.com/showboard/scienprojadc.html

Books:

Bochinski, Julianne, *The Complete Handbook of Science Fair Projects*, 1996.
　　Lists fifty actual projects from past science fairs and suggests procedures without giving away the analyses or results.

Fredericks, Anthony D. and Asimov, Isaac, *The Complete Science Fair Handbook*, 1990.
　　Very helpful book, co-authored by an award-winning science teacher and one of the country's top writers of science fiction and non-fiction.

Kramer, Stephen P., *How to Think like a Scientist*, 1987.
　　A light read on using the scientific method.

Krieger, Melanie Jacobs, *How to Excel in Science Competitions*, 1999.
　　Provides excellent insight into major American science competitions, profiles of students who have become finalists in them.

Rosner, Marc Alan, *Science Fair Success Using the Internet*, 1999.
　　Gives lots of helpful information on communicating safely on the internet, using search tools, and using sources available online to get expert help. Also provides lots of scientific web references organized by science project category such as biology, earth science, and physics.

Van Cleave, Janice, *A Guide to the Best Science Fair Projects*, 1997.
　　She has written numerous books on science experiments and science projects.

Useful web sites – general science & science project information:

You can get listings of helpful web sites by using different combinations of search words like science fair, science project, topic, science teacher, and middle school. Here are some helpful sites to get you started.

Note: Many science teachers and schools have their own science web sites, so use those resources in addition to the ones here.

Cyber-Fair "a resource by and for elementary students." Steps to prepare a science project:
http://www.isd77.k12.mn.us/resources/cf/steps.html

IPL Kid Guide (Internet Public Library) free science fair project resource guide.
http://www.ipl.org/div/kidspace/projectguide/

DiscoverySchool.com, Science fair central: DCYSC's home page for science fairs. Lots of good help and tips for students, teachers, parents, as well as explanation of the nomination process, entry forms, and scholarship information. http://school.discovery.com/sciencefaircentral/

Homeworkspot.com's Science Fair Project Center:
http://www.homeworkspot.com/sciencefair/

California State Science Fair site: Contains lots of links to good resources:
http://www.usc.edu/CSSF/Resources/GettingStarted.html

This web site contains tons of links to educational web sites. Scroll the listing for topics of interest, use the search window, or click on the Science Fairs link.
http://www.science-and-research.com/Science/Educational_Resources/

This cool web site classifies other web sites for K – 12 using the Dewey Decimal System:
http://www.deweybrowse.org/

Try this web site called "The Why Files: science behind the news:" http://whyfiles.org/

YES Mag, Canada's science magazine for kids, has great science topics and hands-on activities and experiments: http://www.yesmag.bc.ca/

Odyssey Magazine's "adventures in science" online site: http://www.odysseymagazine.com/

Useful web sites – specialized sites

Excellent source of information on clouds from the author's all-time favorite college professor and friend: http://www.cloudman.com/

Science Project Ideas from Effortless Gardening. Lots of gardening-related science project ideas plus great tips for students, parents, and educators.
http://www.ergonica.com/ergonica_frame.htm?science_projects_parents.htm&1

Chapter 10

What about next year?

This year's science fair presents great opportunities to prepare for next year.

What opportunities? Here's one: remember how you should identify new questions your project has raised? Well, those questions could become next year's science project, right? That's called *continuation*. Science is like a rolling snowball. The questions just keep building on each other. That's how real science works, so it can work that way for you, too.

High school students often get so engrossed in their science projects that they become year-round research projects. Now that's continuation!

If you do continue your project another year (like the students on p. 45), you'll need to add the ISEF Continuation Projects Form (Form 7) to your packet of entry and approval forms.

The second opportunity comes from just walking around the science fair and looking at the other displays. Think about it: all these students have brought their projects to the same place at the same time. What better place to check other students' ideas and see how they pursued them? Take notes in your journal about things that interest you. It could be a topic, or a way to measure results, or a way to display data. Or you might be interested by new research questions that someone else's project has raised. Who knows? You could get a great idea for next year's project!

If you're lucky enough to go to the regional science fair, or higher, then you get the bonus of seeing even more students' projects. Focus on your own presentation until it's done, but then take time to examine the other projects and talk to the other students.

Chapter 11

How to apply what you've learned in your everyday life

What is a science project all about?

Think about these questions:

1. Which kind of baseball bat will hit a ball farther: a wooden one or a aluminum one?

2. How can you store bananas so they'll stay "fresh" longer – so that they won't turn brown and get mushy so quickly?

3. Which drinking fountains have the most bacteria in your school? In your neighborhood? At the shopping center? Hospital?

4. What effect do different drinks have on your teeth?

5. Is the _____ you see advertised on TV as good as they claim? (You can insert a lot of things in that blank, like toothpaste, laundry detergent, shampoo…sports car.)

Chances are that you don't know the answers to those questions, at least not for sure. But surely you formed an opinion almost as soon as you read some of them. That's good! We often act on opinions and assumptions and things work out just fine.

But how could you test an opinion or assumption to see if the answer you *suppose* is correct, really is? You know the answer, don't you?

You just did that! You can apply the science project process to decisions you make in your everyday life. *Every day!* Don't worry: you don't have to do a full-blown project. Just make the question into a mini-hypothesis, think about how you can test it, and bingo! No one's going to pull a fast one on you.

Just say, "Hmmm. I wonder if what they're saying is true. I could form a hypothesis and test it. Observe the data. See if the data supports the hypothesis, or rejects it. And then decide for myself."

So even if you don't hope to win a science scholarship or become a scientist, you've just learned something for keeps – guaranteed. There are a lot of adults who wish they would have learned that skill when they were in school!

Chapter 12

On Winning

Do you have hopes of doing a winning science project? To be among the finalists at the regional or national science fair? Even try for a scholarship by being one of the top winners at DCYSC or ISEF? If so, then one of your *first* decisions will be one of the most important ones you make. And, once your project is underway, that decision may be difficult or impossible to change in time to meet deadlines.

What is this decision that's so important? It's the topic you choose. As we said in Chapter 1, it should be something you're interested in and it should be neither too hard nor too easy for you to answer. Competition-wise, especially at the middle school level (DCYSC), it also helps if it involves something of practical value. That is, is it likely that your conclusion, when you get there, will be of use to someone? If so, you have a better chance of catching the judges' interest. At the senior high school level (ISEF), judges look for deeper research and are often impressed with students whose conclusions one year open up new questions that can be explored the next year, maybe even a third year.

Some of the questions in the Topic HELPER asked about things like issues in the news or claims made on TV, as well as things of personal interest to you such as hobbies or sports. These are good places to look for topics where you could learn something that would be helpful to others.

Here are some examples of topics from finalists in the 2005 DCYSC:

- Is Seawater an Efficient Medium for Electrolysis: A Model for Solar-powered Hydrogen Production

- What Do You Expect: Does Expectation of Difficulty Level Affect Student Test Performance?

- Hidden Ethyl Alcohol in Soda Pop, Flavored Beverages and Other Food Items

- Will Silicon Help Plant Growth in South Florida Soils?

What else makes a winning project?

In addition to a topic that has practical value, there are two other ingredients for a winning science project: Good science and good communication

If you follow the chapters in Part A of this book, you will have done "good science." As a quick review, good science means that you did these things:

- developed a hypothesis around a clear and plausible relationship between the manipulated and responding variables

- designed and carried out an experiment that tested this relationship in well-controlled conditions

- made a valid conclusion based on your data

- explained any mistakes or challenges that you found along the way

But doing good science isn't enough. It is not enough for science fairs, and it is not enough in the world of scientists, either. You must also be a good communicator of science. The rest of this chapter will cover the communication process step by step, but here's an overall principle: After working out all the tiny details of your project, you must also be able to back up to see the "big picture" view – and be able to tell the story of your project succinctly. And, if you progress from your school's science fair to regional and even national levels, the way you communicate must change along the way. Let's see what this means.

How to be a good communicator of science

As you saw earlier, an important element of scientific research is communicating one's results. Thus, communication is an important element of the judging process at all levels of science fairs. The emphasis may change as you go up to higher levels of competition. Here's how it works using DCYSC as an example:

1. School or local science fair: Display board and written report, and short verbal presentation to the judges.

2. Regional science fair: Same as #1, perhaps with more scientifically experienced judges.

3. Initial DCYSC entry: Answer three written essay questions about the project and submit one visual depiction.

4. DCYSC finalist (top 40 entries): Participate in team challenges. These consist of teamwork and leadership exercises using the scientific method, and oral presentations that are not about the student's project.

Tips for competing at each level of competition

1. School or local science fair

Your visual display must have what's called "curb appeal." In a room full of display boards and apparatus, it should invite the passer-by to stop and look. Keep these tips in mind:
- Use a catchy title.

- Make your headings and key points large enough to be read from a few feet away. Make sure the display looks neat, with enough white space between sections that it looks uncluttered.

- Use one or more photographs to help the viewer visualize your set-up or results.

- Use some variety in color, but don't overdo it. Two or three colors is plenty.

Let your passion for your project show through. This is especially important during the verbal presentation. Are you proud of your experimental design? Excited about your findings? Got great ideas for follow-on research? Then let that excitement come through in your tone of voice and in being eager to answer questions.

2. Regional science fairs

The way you compete at a regional science fair is very similar to the local school fair: You will submit the same display and project report, you'll give a short verbal presentation to judges, and you will answer their questions. Here's a tip to help you prepare: rehearse with someone who isn't familiar with your project, preferably a senior high school or college student or an adult, and preferably someone who's enthusiastic by nature. This will help you in one obvious way and one not-so-obvious:

- The obvious way it helps is to get more practice describing your project and answering questions.

- The not-so-obvious way is that it can regenerate your own excitement in your project – that passion that was mentioned before. By now you've labored for weeks or months with all the details of carrying out the experiment, writing the report, and building the display. And you have lots of other things going on in your life, too. By rehearsing with someone who isn't familiar with your project, you'll catch their excitement as they see what you've done. This helps regenerate your own enthusiasm, and that's what you want the judges to see.

Another tip on dealing with judges: Remember that they are all different, with different levels of intelligence, and different types of expertise in different areas. At the upper levels of competition, you can expect one or more judges to be an expert in the field you are researching, but most of the judges you encounter at the school and regional levels will *not* be experts in your particular field. Thus you must be careful not to be impatient with an adult judge simply because you know more about a topic (or think you do) than he or she does. Always be courteous and never, *never* "talk down" to a judge, no matter how poorly informed they appear to be! In almost all cases, the judge will have looked at your project before you are questioned, so most questions will be related to your methods, your reasonig, and your interpretation of the results. But be prepared for questions that are not specific as well! "Tell me about your project" can be a deadly request if you have not prepared a short, well-rehearsed statement that summarizes what you have done, how you did it, why you did it, and what you found out.

☞ Believe it or not, even charm can be a factor at times. At the 1998 ISEF, a high school senior built a scanning-tunneling electron microscope which he used to experiment with a new method of etching computer chips. But the microscope was housed in Legos and its suspension was provided by bungie cords. Building the actual microscope – not *quite* as difficult as it sounds – showed his engineering skills, and the experiment itself was both valid and imaginative. But the element of charm in the presentation was definitely a factor in drawing judges to this winning project.

3. DCYSC – initial entry

If your project is nominated for DCYSC competition, then that means you've made it to the national level. Congratulations! Someone thinks very highly of your work and your communication ability.

The nature of competition at the DCYSC level is quite different than at the school and regional levels. Instead of display boards and verbal presentations, the first two rounds of competition are conducted without you even being present. Instead, DCYSC uses students' answers to three essay questions to narrow the initial set of entrants – 6,000 students each year – down to 400 semifinalists. Then those same answers are judged again to select 40 finalists who are then flown to Washington, DC, for the final competition.

Here's the web address for the DCYSC:

http://school.discovery.com/sciencefaircentral/dysc/

(Caution: Be sure to check both DCYSC's and ISEF's web sites each year because the entry forms and questions may change from one year to the next.)

Before looking at the specific questions, keep in mind these overall criteria that DCYSC judges use when reviewing entries:

1. Scientific merit & practical value

2. Communication

3. Originality/independent thinking and work

DCSYC asks specific questions to which the student must supply short essay answers. There is a word limit for each answer. Be sure to get the actual entry forms from DCYSC's web site. Here is a brief summary to help you "see" the big picture of what they're asking for:

1. Overview of project (500 word limit, which is about two pages, double spaced)

    a. How did you get your idea?
    b. Who else helped, and how?
    c. What was your hypothesis or question?
    d. Give an overview of your experimental procedures
    e. Did you face any special challenges?
    f. Was your hypothesis accepted or rejected? Why?

2. Visual image (You may submit a one-page image – photograph, diagram, or drawing – to go along with your essays.)

3. Overall results (250 words, or about one typed page)

    a. 1 or 2 key things you learned
    b. Any surprises, and how did you deal with them?
    c. If you could do it over, how could you improve it? Why?
    d. Did your results raise any new questions you could explore?

    4. Relevance and creative writing (500 words, or about two typed pages)

        a. Write an article* explaining its usefulness, or
        b. Describe any presentations you've given on your project

* Answer the questions who, what, when, where, why, and how about the significance of your findings to others.

These steps may help you answer the above questions.

1. Do some brainstorming. Give yourself about two minutes to write down as many ideas as you can under each question. Work fast. Write every idea that comes to mind, no matter how off-beat it might seem at first. Don't take time to evaluate your ideas yet, just get them down on paper.

2. Then go back and circle or highlight the ideas that seem most useable for each question.

3. Create an outline. The sub-questions under DCYSC's questions above are a good starting point for outlining the story of your project. Organize the useable ideas from your brainstorming session under each of those sub-questions. As you do this you may need to fill in some gaps in order to tell your project's story logically.

4. Write a rough draft for each question. Don't worry about length or spelling yet. Instead, concentrate on telling your project's story clearly and logically.

5. Once you like the overall flow of your answers, then see if you meet the word limits for each question (500, 250, and 500 for questions #1, 2, and 4, respectively). Too long? Look first for unneeded adjectives or phrases. Here's an example: Instead of saying, "The first topic that I came up with needed to be refined…" [12 words], say this: "My first topic had to be refined…" [7 words]. Remember, the purpose of these questions is to see who can communicate the key elements of their research in a limited amount of space.

5. DCYSC finalist competition. The nature of this competition may vary each year. For example, in 2003, the 40 finalists in the Discovery Channel Youth Science Challenge were brought to Washington, DC, for the final competition. Also, that year the competition didn't relate directly to each student's project. Instead, students were given various science scenarios and were judged on their teamwork, leadership, and overall science communication skills. If you make it this far, there is little you can do to prepare for this final competition. It pretty much depends on what's inside you at that point.

Chapter 13

Teacher's Corner

The purpose of this chapter is to share a few tips from seasoned science teachers and list some teacher resources on the internet. Here are some key tips:

o Encourage students to select a **topic** that is personally meaningful to them. In sports they call this "having some skin in the game." This keeps them motivated.

o The single most important factor in science project success, especially at the middle school level, is **direct adult involvement** by a knowledgeable person such as a parent, you (but you're spread thin), or a mentor. This adult's role is to listen and advise, not steer or do the student's work.

• **Start early** and do **parallel exercises** to help students prepare for certain key steps. There are some suggestions and references in this chapter for exercises to help students state a hypothesis and develop procedures. You may want to add your own exercises for logical thinking, analyzing data, and evaluating results.

• Be careful **not to overwhelm** students. Give them instructions one step at a time.

• **Identify students who are ready** vs. those who aren't. One way to approach this is to require a commitment months in advance of the presentation date. Check progress along the way to see who appears to have the staying power, and that all-important parental involvement.

• Help **connect students with mentors.** Almost all successful science fair projects involve significant mentorshiops with professors, professional scientists and engineers, and other experts. Students are almost always intimidated by the idea of presenting their project concept to a professional in their field of research, so help them make the connection. *Tip:* Your local or regional science fair director will have a list of mentors who have worked with students of all ages. No student is too young to ask questions that only an expert can answer fully!

• Help your students **manage their time.** At a minimum, science projects span several weeks and involve a blend of steps and skills like no other school assignment. It may help to give your students a checklist like the one below so they and you can plan and track their progress.

Project Steps	Description	Com-pleted?	Teacher approved?
Experimental question	Find a topic that interests you and write an experimental question in the form: "How does _____ affect _____?" where the first blank holds the manipulated variable and the second holds the responding variable.		
Collect research	Find information about your manipulated and responding variables, including information about any research that has been done previously.		
Research report/rough draft	Write the important information in your own words.		
Hypothesis	What you believe will happen in your experiment and why (based on your research)		
Materials/Procedure	A list of materials you need and a step-by-step procedure describing exactly what you will do to test your hypothesis		
Testing	Do your experiment according to your procedure.		
Research report/final copy	Important information word processed or written neatly in ink and spell-checked.		
Organize and present data	A data table and/or graph of experimental results.		
Conclusion	What do you conclude about your hypothesis from your data? · answer the experimental question based on results · discussion of the reliability of your results · why this information is useful · suggestions for further research		
Display	These parts of the experiment should be presented in an attractive visual display.		
Prepare for presentation	Write notes on 3 x 5 index cards and practice what you will say when you present to the class.		

Adapted from the Kids Guide to Science Projects website of the Tucson (AZ) Unified School District.

There is an annual cycle that will influence when you conduct your local science fair. School fairs feed into regional fairs, then state and national. For DCYSC (5th to 8th graders), the entry deadline is around June 4th, so local schools often hold their science fairs in the

Spring. For ISEF (high school), regional science fairs are usually held in February, so local science fairs must be held earlier. Whether you're affiliated with DCYSC or ISEF, it's not a bad idea to announce the science project assignment early in the school year so students can start thinking about their topic and question.

Both DCYSC and ISEF accept team projects of two to three students. Consider teaming if 1) synergy between two students will yield a better project (for example, you might team a good scientific thinker with a good communicator) or 2) you want to enable more students to get experience at the regional level. Note that the DCYSC entry form requires an explanation of how the project was improved by a team vs. one individual.

Know which fair your school is affiliated with (DCYSC or ISEF), and which rules apply. Students will need to adhere to those rules starting from the point when they're designing their procedures and getting proper permission to proceed.

There are other science competitions, some of which offer the winners sizable scholarships. See the ISEF home page for some of the possibilities.

Teacher resources on the web

Your students may benefit from exercises that prepare them for certain steps in the science project process such as developing hypotheses and procedures. (See the note from Ken Newkirk at the end of this chapter.) The GEMS web site is a popular source of such exercises: http://www.lhs.berkeley.edu/GEMS/gemspubs.html

Here's a complete (and fun) exercise from NASA on developing hypotheses, provided for those without web access. For those with access, the NASA link is http://scifiles.larc.nasa.gov/.

Writing a Hypothesis

Directions

Create a hypothesis statement for each of the situations below using the If-then format. (If = the CAUSE; then = the EFFECT.)

A **hypothesis** is an estimate or "educated guess" for solving a problem based on facts, observations, and available data.

- **Example Scenario:** A student wants to see if the amount of sunlight affects the growth cycle of a pansy. The student places one pansy on a window sill (natural light) and another in the living room (only artificial light).

Hypothesis: *If* a pansy is placed in natural light *then* it will grow two inches higher than a pansy grown in the artificial light.

Situation 1

A sanitation department is nearby and the smell is coming from the same direction. The sanitation department does a series of steps to process the sewage and waste water.

Hypothesis: If _____

then _____

Situation 2

The tree house detectives want to see if different smells travel at the same speed. They spray a can of hairspray, peppermint air freshener, and insect repellant at the same time. Six friends stand around them in a large circle, five feet from the center of the circle where the three tree house detectives stood.

Hypothesis: If _____

then _____

Situation 3

The tree house detectives want to know if the candy making process affects the odor given off by the candy. To conduct the experiment, they help Dr. D make orange taffy candy.

Hypothesis: If _____

then _____

- -

Answer Key

Scenario 1: If the wind blows from the direction of the sanitation department, then the smell released from the sewage and wastewater will be carried with the wind.

Scenario 2: If each of the three tree house detectives sprays an aerosol can (hair spray, peppermint air freshener, or insect repellent) at the same time from the center of a circle, then the five people standing around the circle will be able to simultaneously smell the three scents from a distance of five feet.

If each of the three tree house detectives sprays an aerosol can (hair spray, peppermint air freshener, or insect repellent) at the same time from the center of a circle, then the air freshener will travel five feet away from the center of the circle and be detected first, followed by the insect spray, and finally by the hair spray.

If each of the three tree house detectives sprays an aerosol can (hair spray, peppermint air freshener, or insect repellent) at the same time from the center of a circle, then the hair spray will travel five feet away from the center of the circle and be detected first.

If each of the three tree house detectives sprays an aerosol can (hair spray, peppermint air freshener, or insect repellent) at the same time from the center of a circle, then none of the three scents will be detected by their friends standing five feet away from the center of the circle.

Scenario 3: If the tree house detectives and Dr. D make orange taffy according to the official candy factory process, then they will confirm that no new odors are given off.

If the tree house detectives and Dr. D make orange taffy by increasing the cooking time of the mixture, then they will find different and/or unpleasant odors are given off.

If the tree house detectives and Dr. D make orange taffy by increasing the amount of artificial flavoring, then the orange smell of the candy will become stronger.

Other science-related web resources for teachers

http://scienceteacherstuff.com/natureofscience.html
    Science Teacher Stuff, resources for K-12, has lots of links to good resources for teachers, including how to teach certain topics.

http://www.nal.usda.gov/Kids/scimags.htm
    National Agricultural Library's Kids' Science Page. Lots of links including a list of science magazines for kids.

http://www.cascience.org
    California Science Teacher's Association website of resources. Lots of great science links for teachers and students including science education suppliers, resources, web links, and regional California information.

http://www.educationplanet.com/
    Education Planet, "the education web guide."

Several experienced science teachers contributed ideas to this book. Here are observations and advice from one of them:[14]

    The 8th and 9th grade teachers in my district take from 6-8 weeks to complete a science project, working nearly 5 one-hour class periods per week during that time. This even involves a week or so for presentations by students to the class and peer grading, etc.

---

14. Quoted from an e-mail dated Feb. 25, 2003, from Mr. Ken Newkirk, teacher in the Selah School District, Washinton State. Used by permission.

Those of us working with 6th and 7th graders find it takes longer. My situation is unusual as I only see a student one full day per week (in a pull-out class). Twelve year olds CANNOT and should not work on a science project all day long, so we usually spend 2 hours (3 at most during "crunch time.") So it takes us about 18-20 weeks (or days—however you want to look at it.)

Prior to even discussing a manipulated science project, students need classroom experience with hands-on science in which a hypothesis is generated and tested under the direction of a teacher. My 6th graders test the strength and absorbency of paper towels and the vitamin C content of various juices as classroom activities before we ever start their projects. My 7th graders do a comparison of resting versus exercising heart rate in class. Another 6th grade teacher does a big unit on pendulums trying to determine which variables change swing frequency. (Good sources for these types of activities are the "GEMS" guides produced by the Lawrence Hall of Science. http://www.lhs.berkeley.edu/GEMS/gemspubs.html)

You ask about encouraging planning and patience in the students. It is easy to scare students if you show them everything that will eventually be required. On the other hand you have to give them a clear image of the target and the process. It is a delicate balancing act. Usually I give them a packet... that shows all the steps and discuss it for 10-20 minutes. Then I immediately jump into the phase of selecting a topic. I try to make them focus on only the task at hand and put their energy and worry into just that one thing for today. Occasionally we revisit the full list of steps, but not often and never for very long.

I will close by saying that selecting a good topic is critical and is probably the hardest part for most children. . . The next hardest part is writing good procedures: inclusion of all major steps, adequate details, correct ordering, understandable wording, etc. Writing the procedures is hard to do and harder to teach.

Appendix A

Part 1 - Topic ideas and categories

For a complete list of science project categories, consult the Intel ISEF Research Categories web page at http://www.sciserv.org/isef/primer/research_categories.asp

Here is a list of the categories that seem to be chosen most often:

• **Behavioral and social sciences** – human and animal behavior and relationships. Any work with people or vertebrate animals requires permission from such sources as parents, your principal, doctors or veterinarians, and finally, the Institutional Review Board of ISEF before you can begin your experiment.

• **Botany** – study of plants (and molds and fungus for science project purposes).

• **Chemistry** – nature and composition of matter such as materials, plastics, pesticides, soft drinks.

• **Environmental Science** – pollution of air, water, or land: sources and their control. Wherever you live, there is probably an environmental issue that you can explore.

• **Medicine and Health** – diseases and health of humans and animals: dentistry, nutrition, allergies, skin care, hearing, etc.

• **Physics** – motion and energy; effect of energy on matter, including light and optics, sound, particles, fluids and gasses. Simple machines, electricity, power, motion, heat, magnetism.

• **Zoology** – animals and insects. If vertebrate animals will be involved, then you'll need special permission before you begin your experiment.

This author recommends that students start with their own areas of interest, then identify a research question that is personally meaningful. However, it is sometimes helpful to scan lists of project topics or titles for ideas. The rest of this appendix contains some examples. If you don't find what you're looking for here, there are dozens of books and web sites with such lists.

One such site is the Science Fairs Home Page from the Eastern Newfoundland Science Fairs Council. Below is a condensed list of their project ideas for Grades 7 to 9, listed by category. The complete list is available at http://www.stemnet.nf.ca/sciencefairs/

PHYSICS

- Fire and Burning – what factors affect burning?
- Fuels and their efficiency in producing energy.
- Musical instruments – the scientific principles behind them
- Pendulums – how can a period of a pendulum be increased?
- Gears – compare efficiencies, effect of different lubricants
- Solar Furnace
- Lenses – effects of curvature, materials on light beams
- How strong are nylon fishing lines?
- What factors affect the bounce of a dropped ball?
- How strong is a toothpick?
- Which type of lawn sprinkler works best?
- Which type\size of light bulb produces the most light?
- Which materials can be charged with static electricity?
- Which battery lasts the longest? – How can power be increased?
- What affects light reflection? – refraction and diffraction of light?
- What affects the pitch of sound? – What affects the volume of sound? How would you measure the velocity of sound?
- Electric Motors – principles and factors effecting their efficiency

ENGINEERING\PHYSICS

- Use of solar energy – design and construct solar cookers, solar panels, etc.
- Designing a strong bridge, or an energy efficient home
- Efficient use of renewable energy resources – for example, wood, wind
- Determine the accuracy of various thermometers
- Principle of energy conservation

METEOROLOGY

- Snow – what happens when it melts; what does it contain; structure of snow flakes; life in a snow bank
- Sky Color – account for differences in color at different times
- Wind and Clouds – what are the common wind patterns in your area and why? Is cloud formation related to height, weather systems and temperature? Study and record how clouds relate to weather patterns.
- Water levels – study and record varying levels over the year in a body of water; account for differences and the results on the surrounding environment.
- Dew formation – how much is formed on a square meter for a period of time; account for variations

- Wind – does wind travel at same speeds and in same directions at different heights?
- Frost formation – what must the temperature be to form first; what are the effects of humidity? What is the make – up of frost and dew?
- Evaporation – which effects the rate of evaporation most – temperature, humidity, wind speed or other factors?
- Rain – can you measure the speed and force of raindrops? – What is the effect on soil, with and without ground cover? Could you simulate the effect of rain?
- Heat Retention – does fresh water hold heat longer than salt water? How does water compare to land and what effect does this have on the weather? What factors affect the cooling of land?
- Sunlight – how do different surfaces affect the amount of sunlight reflected and absorbed? Design a method of measuring how much sunshine is available each day.
- Weather records – Design and build an automatic recording weather device. Test it over a period of time.
- Effects of Humidity – what happens to hair during periods of changing humidity?

CHEMISTRY

- Everyday activities that illustrate chemical principles
- Chemical reactions that produce energy or that require energy
- Testing of consumer products – glues, stain removers, antiseptics, mouthwash, detergents, paper towels, making salt water potable, removal of pollutants
- Effects of sunlight on rubber, ink, paper
- Compare the pH levels in mouths of various animals and humans at different times in the day
- Compare the surface tension of various liquids
- Dealing with chemical spills from industry
- Analyzing snow and rain for pollutants; samples from different locations
- Effects of temperature on density of gases
- Effects of salt and other contaminants on rate of rusting
- Growing crystals – factors that affect the rate and the size
- Can you obtain water from ink, vinegar, milk?
- Analyze soil samples for their components, ability to hold moisture, fertility and pH
- Does the amount of particle pollution vary with distance from a road, with location, with height. Determine types of particles found in pollution fallout
- Fire extinguishers – principles of operation and factors affecting their efficient use
- How do acids react with different metals under varying conditions
- Identify different metals by the color of flame when they burn
- Electroplating – the principles, how different metals can be used and the practical applications

BOTANY

(Note: some teachers discourage experiments involving plants because they often seem doomed to catastrophe. Just so you know.)

- Germination – how monocots and dicots differ – the effects of heat, light, carbon dioxide, pH level, etc. on germination rate
- Photosynthesis – factors affecting the rate of photosynthesis temperature, light intensity, water, carbondioxide – part of light spectrum used in photosynthesis
- Leaf – do the numbers and sizes of stomata vary with different plants – what happens if stomata are covered and why?
- Roots – how much water is used by different plants – what is the effect of temperature, sunlight, etc., on the use of water (transpiration) – how do different types of soils affect the ability of roots to anchor plants – what factors encourage root growth and what is the effect of water, oxygen, soil type, minerals on root growth
- Plant growth – determine the effects of various nutrients, amounts of water, hours of sunlight, strength of weed killer, temperature, pollutants, pH levels on plant growth and crop yields – can plants live without oxygen, carbon dioxide – what percentages of various plants is water
- Genetic Studies – connections between hair and eye color, sex and left handedness, hair color and strength – family studies on inheritance
- What conditions are favorable for: – fungus growth – E.G. yeast, mold, mildew diseases – mushroom production – growing brine shrimp – algae growth – bacteria growth or control – mutations – rooting cuttings – the survival of Planaria – the growth of nitrogen fixing bacteria – lichen growth
- Field Studies – effects of herbicide spraying, acid rain in a lake, auto exhausts on a roadside, SO2 emissions on plants, under hydro lines – types of bacteria found around the home, on the body, in soil of different types
- Reactions of protozoa to changes in the environment
- The preferred pH level in the soil for various plants

Appendix B

Approval forms and science fair information

This appendix contains three sections:

1. Information about approval forms
2. General information about science fairs and how to enter them
3. Printouts of ISEF approval forms (The 2006-2007 forms in this edition of *Science Project Helper*. Although ISEF forms vary only slightly from year to year, the forms included here should be used as guides only.)

1. Information about approval forms

Step 3d (p. 28) discussed the approval process required before you begin your actual experiment. Many elementary and middle schools use simplified versions of ISEF forms (International Science and Engineering Fair). Your teacher or science director will provide you with these forms at the appropriate phase of your project.

If your school uses the actual ISEF approval forms, the ISEF web site has a rules wizard that can help you determine which forms you need depending on specific aspects of your project. Here's the link:

http://www.sciserv.org/isef/students/wizard/index.asp

Pages 82 –98 include a table and sample ISEF forms for 2007 so you can see what kind of information they require. **CAUTION:** *Always check the DCYSC or ISEF web sites for up-to-date forms and guidance on which forms you will need for your project.*

2. General information about science fairs and how to enter them

If your project wins an award at your school's science fair, you may be asked to compete at the district or regional level, and then if you win there, all the way to national fairs! Several scholarships are awarded at those levels, so a really great project could really pay off! For example, at the national level for middle school students there are several $500 scholarships and the winner wins a $15,000 scholarship.)

Most middle schools – 5th to 8th grade – are affiliated with the Discovery Channel Young Scientists Challenge (DCYSC), whereas most high schools – 9th to 12th grade – are affiliated with the International Science and Engineering Fair (ISEF).

If you do go on to regional or district science fairs, your teacher will help you get the entry forms (which are different from the approval forms mentioned in Step 3d and in part 1 of this Appendix).

Both DCYSC and ISEF are run by an organization called Science Service. Check their website for DCYSC and ISEF rules, entry forms, and other information: http://www.sciserv.org/.

NOTE: *Be sure you're using the current year's rules and forms as Science Service updates them periodically.* You can also call Science Service at 202-785-2255 or write to Science Service, 1719 N St., NW, Washington, DC 20036.

You should know one more thing about entering science fairs. If your project is selected for regional or higher competition and you didn't use ISEF approval forms, don't despair. DCYSC will not penalize you for using different forms, but they do need to see evidence that you had the proper supervision, pre-approval, and informed consent. This includes your teacher's written approval before you started your actual experiment, and any paperwork you completed if you worked with human subjects, vertebrate animals, tissue, pathogens or recombinant DNA, or controlled or hazardous materials. If you *are* going on to another level of competition, however, it is a good idea to fill out a set of the official ISEF forms in addition to the ones you used from your school. This can be confusing since several are for pre-approval of research! For those forms, do not have them signed after the fact! Just attach your origional school forms.

ABOUT THE FOLLOWING FORMS:
Pages 83-98 contain the 2007 ISEF forms. They are reproduced here slightly reduced in size. You must download the actual forms from http://www.sciserv.org. *You can also obtain them by writing to Science Service, 1719 N St., NW, Washington, DC 20036. Always check the DCYSC or ISEF web sites for up-to-date forms and guidance on which forms you will need for your project.*

For more information, you can also check the website for this book:
http://www.scienceprojecthelper.com

USING THE CORRECT FORMS

Which project...	... needs these ISEF Forms?
1. <u>All</u> projects need these forms, dated and signed <u>before</u> experimentation begins:	• Checklist for Adult Sponsor/Safety Assessment Form (1) • Student Checklist (1A) • Research Plan Attachment • Research Plan • Approval Form (1B)
2. In addition, you must submit additional forms for any of the situations listed below:	
➤ Team project?	• Research Plan (1A) – Team
➤ Will you be doing your project in a registered research institution (like a university or medical center)?	• Registered Research Institutional/Industrial Setting form (1C) (Completed <u>after</u> the experimentation)
➤ Will your project involve vertebrate animals, people, dangerous or controlled substances, or human tissue such as blood and teeth?	• Qualified Scientist Form (2) signed <u>before</u> experimentation begins • Risk Assessment Form (3) for all projects involving Hazardous Chemicals, Activities or Devices AND whichever of these applies, signed <u>before</u> experimentation begins: • Human Subjects and Informed Consent Form (4) • Vertebrate Animal Form (5) • Hazardous Risk Assessment Form (6A) • Human and Vertebrate Animal Tissue Form (6B)
Project being continued from previous year?	• Continuation Projects Form (7) Note: attach previous year's abstract and Research Plan with attachments

Checklist for Adult Sponsor (1)
This completed form is required for ALL projects and must be completed prior to experimentation

To be completed by the Adult Sponsor in collaboration with the student researcher:

Student's Name: _____

Project Title: _____

1) ☐ I have reviewed the ISEF Rules and Guidelines.

2) ☐ I have reviewed the student's completed Student Checklist (1A) and Research Plan.

3) ☐ I have worked with the student and we have discussed the possible risks involved in the project.

4) ☐ The project involves one or more of the following and requires prior approval by an SRC, IRB, IACUC (

    ☐ Humans   ☐ Potentially Hazardous Biological Agents

    ☐ Vertebrate Animals   ☐ Microorganisms   ☐ rDNA   ☐ Tissues

5) Forms to be completed for ALL Projects:

    ☐ Adult Sponsor Checklist (1)   ☐ Research Plan

    ☐ Student Checklist (1A)   ☐ Approval Form (1B)

        ☐ Regulated Research Institutional/Industrial Setting Form (1C) (when applicable)

        ☐ Continuation Form (7) (when applicable)

6) Additional forms required if the project includes the use of one or more of the following (check all that apply):

☐ **Humans** (Requires prior approval by an Institutional Review Board (IRB), see pp. 13-16 for full text of the rules)

    ☐ Human Subjects Form (4)

    ☐ Qualified Scientist Form (2) (if applicable and/or required by the IRB)

☐ **Vertebrate Animals** (Requires prior approval, see pp. 17-20 for full text of the rules)

    ☐ Vertebrate Animal Form (5A) - for projects conducted in a non-regulated research site (SRC prior approval required.)

    ☐ Vertebrate Animal Form (5B) - for projects conducted at a Regulated Research Institution. (Institutional Animal Care and Use Committee (IACUC) approval required prior experimentation.)

    ☐ Qualified Scientist Form (2) (Required for all vertebrate animal projects at a regulated research site or when applicable)

☐ **Potentially Hazardous Biological Agents** (Requires prior approval by SRC, IACUC or Institutional Biosafety Committee (IBC), see pp. 21-24 for full text of the rules.)

    ☐ Potentially Hazardous Biological Agents Form (6A)

    ☐ Human and Vertebrate Animal Tissue Form (6B) - to be completed in addition to Form 6A when project involves the use of fresh tissue, primary cell cultures, blood, blood products and body fluids.

    ☐ Qualified Scientist Form (2) (when applicable)

☐ **Hazardous Chemicals, Activities and Devices** (No prior approval required, see pp.25-27 for full text of the rules.)

    ☐ Risk Assessment Form (3)

    ☐ Qualified Scientist Form (2) (required for projects involving DEA-controlled substances or when applicable)

_____ _____ _____
Adult Sponsor's Printed Name   Signature   Date of Review
                                                      (Must be prior to experimentation.)

_____ _____
Phone   Email

International Rules 2006/2007   full text of the rules and electronic copies of forms are available at www.sciserv.org/isef

Page 29

Student Checklist (1A)

This completed form is required for ALL individual projects.
Complete all sections by printing or typing all information requested.

1) Student's Name: _____ Grade: _____

   Email: _____ Phone: _____

2) Title of Project: _____

3) School: _____ School Phone: _____

   School Address: _____

4) Adult Sponsor: _____ Phone/Email: _____

5) Is this a continuation from a previous year? ☐ Yes   ☐ No
   If Yes:
   a) Attach the previous year's ☐ **Abstract**   ☐ **Form 1A and**   ☐ **Research Plan**
   b) Explain how this project is new and different from previous years on ☐ **Continuation Form (7)**

6) **This year's** laboratory experiment/data collection will begin: (must be stated (mm/dd/yy)

   Projected Start Date: _____ Projected End Date: _____

   ACTUAL Start Date: _____ ACTUAL End Date: _____

7) Where will you conduct your experimentation? (check all that apply)
   ☐ Research Institution   ☐ School   ☐ Field   ☐ Home   ☐ Other: _____

8) List name and address of all non-school work site(s):

   Name: _____   _____

   Address: _____   _____

   _____   _____

   Phone: _____   _____

9) **Complete a Research Plan (See page 32) and attach to this form.**

10) **An abstract is required for all projects after experimentation (see page 28).**

International Rules 2006/2007   full text of the rules and electronic copies of forms are available at www.sciserv.org/isef

Page 30

Student Checklist (1A) - TEAM

This completed form is required for ALL team projects.
Complete all sections by printing or typing all information requested.

1) a. Team Leader: _____ Grade: _____

   b. Team Member: _____ c. Team Member _____

   Email: _____ Phone: _____

2) Title of Project: _____

3) School: _____ School Phone: _____

   School Address: _____

4) Adult Sponsor: _____ Phone/Email: _____

5) Is this a continuation from a previous year? ☐ Yes ☐ No
   If Yes:
   a) Attach the previous year's ☐ **Abstract** ☐ **Form 1A and** ☐ **Research Plan**
   b) Explain how this project is new and different from previous years on ☐ **Continuation Form (7)**

6) **This year's** laboratory experiment/data collection will begin: **(must be stated (mm/dd/yy)**

   Projected Start Date: _____ Projected End Date: _____

   ACTUAL Start Date: _____ ACTUAL End Date: _____

7) Where will you conduct your experimentation? (check all that apply)
   ☐ Research Institution ☐ School ☐ Field ☐ Home ☐ Other: _____

8) List name and address of all non-school work site(s):

   Name: _____   _____

   Address: _____   _____

   _____   _____

   Phone: _____   _____

9) **Complete a Research Plan (See page 32) and attach to this form.**

10) **An abstract is required for all projects after experimentation (see page 28).**

Internuational Rules 2006/2007   full text of the rules and electronic copies of forms are available at www.sciserv.org/isef

Page 31

Research Plan

REQUIRED for ALL Projects
A complete research plan must accompany Checklist for Student (1A)

Provide a typed research plan and attach to Checklist for Students (1A).

The research plan for all projects is to include the following:

A. Question being addressed

B. Hypothesis/Problem/Engineering Goals

C. Description in detail of method or procedures (The following are important and key items that should be included when formulating ANY AND ALL research plans. These are guidelines and should be followed where applicable. *Refer to Items 1-4 below.)

All Projects
- **Procedures:** Detail all procedures and experimental design to be used for data collection
- **Data Analysis:** Describe the procedures you will use to analyze the data that answer research question or hypothesis
- **Bibliography:** List at least five (5) major references (e.g. science journal articles, books, internet sites) from your library research. If you plan to use vertebrate animals, give an additional animal care reference.
    - Choose one style and use it consistently to reference the literature used in the research plan
        - Guidelines can be found in the Student Handbook and any Research Journal under the "Instructions to Authors"

1. **Human subjects research** (See instructions on p 13 of the International Rules):
    - Detail all procedures, include what the participants are asked to do (see p. 13)
    - Describe Risk Assessment process and how risks will be minimized
    - Describe Study Sample/Participants
        - Number of participants and estimated participants demographics (may include information such as: age, male/female, cultural background breakdown, Socio-economic status)
        - Recruitment procedures (where and how subjects are recruited)
        - Procedures for obtaining informed consent if applicable, include statement about informing potential participants about voluntary nature of participation and right to withdraw at any time
        - Strategies used to protect privacy and confidentiality
    - Include survey or questionnaires if used, and critically evaluate the risk
        - List and describe the measures (questionnaires, surveys) used and how you measure the variable of interest (behavioral observations, time, length). Attach the questionnaire/survey
        - Consider emotional stress and potential consequences
    - Describe any physical activities or procedures, if used, and critically evaluate the risks
        - Type, duration of exercise or physical activity
        - Ingestion method, amount, intervals, etc.

2. **Vertebrate animal research** (See instructions on p.17 of the International Rules):
    - Briefly discuss **POTENTIAL ALTERNATIVES** and present a detailed justification for use of vertebrate animals
    - Explain potential impact or contribution this research may have
    - Detail all procedures to be used
        - Include methods used to minimize potential discomfort, distress, pain and injury to the animals during the course of experimentation
        - Detailed chemical concentrations and drug dosages
    - Detail animal numbers, species, strain, sex, age, etc.
        - Include justification of the numbers planned for the research
    - Describe housing and oversight of daily care
    - Discuss disposition of the animals at the termination of the study

3. **Potentially Hazardous Biological Agents** (See instructions on p.21 of the International Rules):
    - Describe Biosafety Level Assessment process and resultant BSL determination
    - Give source of agent
    - Detail safety precautions
    - Discuss methods of disposal

4. **Hazardous Chemicals, Activities & Devices** (See instructions on p.25 of the International Rules):
    - Describe Risk Assessment process and results
    - Detail chemical concentrations and drug dosages
    - Describe safety precautions and procedures to minimize risk
    - Discuss methods of disposal

International Rules 2006/2007   **full text of the rules and electronic copies of forms are available at www.sciserv.org/isef**

Page 32

Approval Form (1B)
This completed form is required for ALL projects.

1) REQUIRED FOR ALL PROJECTS.

a) Student Acknowedgment:

☐ I understand the risks and possible dangers to me of the proposed research plan. I have read the ISEF Rules and Guidelir will adhere to all International Rules when conducting this research.

☐ I have read and will abide by the following Ethics statement:

Scientific fraud and misconduct are not condoned at any level of research or competition. Such practices include plag rism, forgery, use or presentation of other researcher's work as one's own, and fabrication of data. Fraudulent proje will fail to qualify for competition in affiliated fairs or the ISEF.

_____ _____ _____
Student's Printed Name   Signature   Date Acknowledged
                                                                                             (Must be prior to experimentation.)

b) Parent/Guardian Approval: I have read and understand the risks and possible dangers involved in the **Research Plan**. I consent to my child participating in this research.

_____ _____ _____
Parent/Guardian's Printed Name   Signature   Date of Approval
                                                                                             (Must be prior to experimentation.)

2) TO BE COMPLETED BY THE SRC
(REQUIRED FOR PROJECTS REQUIRING PRIOR SRC/IRB APPROVAL. SIGN 2a OR 2b AS APPROPRIATE.)

a) Required for projects that need prior SRC/ IRB approval BEFORE experimentation		**b) Required for research conducted at all Regulated Research Institutions with no prior fair SRC/IRB approval.**
(humans, vertebrates or potentially hazardous biological agents)		This project was conducted at a regulated research institution (**not home or high school, etc.**), was reviewed and approved by the proper institutional board before experimentation and complies with the ISEF Rules. **Attach (1C) and required institutional approvals (e.g. IACUC, IRB)**
The SRC/IRB has carefully studied this project's **Research Plan** and all the required forms are included. My signature indicates approval of the **Research Plan** before the student begins experimentation.	**OR**	
_____ SRC/IRB Chair's Printed Name		_____ SRC/IRB Chair's Printed Name
_____ _____ Signature Date of Approval (Must be prior to experimentation.)		_____ _____ Signature Date of Approval

NOTE: If a stamp is used, it <u>must</u> be initialed by the chairperson.

3) FINAL ISEF AFFILIATED FAIR SRC APPROVAL.   (REQUIRED FOR ALL PROJECTS)

SRC Approval After Experimentation and Shortly Before Competition at Regional/State/National Fair
I certify that this project adheres to the approved **Research Plan** and complies with all ISEF Rules.

_____ _____ _____
Regional SRC Chair's Printed Name   Signature   Date of Approval

_____ _____ _____
State/National SRC Chair's Printed Name Signature   Date of Approval
(where applicable)

Regulated Research Institutional/Industrial Setting Form (1C)
This form must be completed by the scientist supervising the student research conducted in a regu research institution (*e.g.*, universities, medical centers, NIH, etc.) or industrial setting.

This form MUST be displayed with your project.

Student's Name _____

Title of Project _____

To be completed by the Scientist (NOT the Student or Adult Sponsor) after experimentation:

The student conducted research at my institution: (check one)

a) ☐ only to use the equipment   b) ☐ to perform experiment(s)/conduct research

1) How did the student get the idea for her/his project?
   (e.g. Was the project assigned, picked from a list, an original student idea, etc.)

2) Were you made aware of the ISEF rules before experimentation?   ☐ Yes   ☐ No

3) Did the student work on the project as a part of a research group?   ☐ Yes   ☐ No
   If yes, how large was the group and what kind of research group was it (students, group of adult researchers, etc.)

4) What specific procedures or equipment did the student actually use and how independently did the student work
   Please list and describe. (Do not list procedures student **only** observed.)

Student research projects dealing with human subjects, vertebrate animals or potentially hazardous biological agents require review and approval by an institutional regulatory board (IRB/IACUC/IBC). **Copy of approval(s) must be attached.**

_____   _____   _____
Scientist's Printed Name   Signature   Title

_____   _____
Institution   Date Signed

_____   _____
Address   Email/ Phone

Qualified Scientist Form (2)

May be required for research involving human subjects, vertebrate animals, potentially hazardous biolog agents, and DEA-controlled Substances. Must be completed and signed prior to the start of student experimentation.

Student's Name _____

Title of Project _____

To be completed by the Qualified Scientist:

Scientist Name: _____

Educational Background: _____ Degree(s): _____
Experience/Training as relates to the student's area of research:

_____

Position: _____ Institution: _____

Address: _____ Email/Phone: _____

1) Were you made aware of the ISEF rules before student experimentation? ☐ yes ☐ no

2) Will any of the following be used?

   a) Human subjects . . . . ☐ yes ☐ no

   b) Vertebrate animals . . . . ☐ yes ☐ no

   c) Potentially hazardous biological agents (microorganisms, rDNA and tissues, including blood and blood products) . . . . ☐ yes ☐ no
   . . . . .

   d) DEA-classed substances. . . . . ☐ yes ☐ no

3) Will you directly supervise the student? . . . . ☐ yes ☐ no

   a. If no, who will directly supervise and serve as the Designated Supervisor? _____

   b. Experience/Training of the Designated Supervisor:

4) Describe the safety precautions and training necessary for this project:

To be completed by the Qualified Scientist:	To be completed by the Designated Supervisor when the Qualified Scientist cannot directly supervise
I certify that I have reviewed and approved the **Research Plan** prior to the start of the experimentation. If the student or Designated Supervisor is not trained in the necessary procedures, I will ensure her/his training. I will provide advice and supervision during the research. I have a working knowledge of the techniques to be used by the student in the **Research Plan**. I understand that a Designated Supervisor is required when the student is not conducting experimentation under my direct supervision.	I certify that I have reviewed the **Research Plan** and have been trained in the techniques to be used by this student, and I will provide direct supervision.
_____ Qualified Scientist's Printed Name	_____ Designated Supervisor's Printed Name
_____ _____ Signature Date of Approval	_____ _____ Signature Date of Approval
	_____ _____ Phone Email

International Rules 2006/2007 **full text of the rules and electronic copies of forms are available at www.sciserv.org/isef**

Page 35

Risk Assessment Form (3)

Required for projects using hazardous chemicals, activities or devices or regulated substances. Must be completed prior to student experimentation.

Student's Name _____

Title of Project _____

To be completed by the Student Researcher in collaboration with Designated Supervisor/Qualit tist:

(All questions must be answered; additional page(s) may be attached.)
1. List/identify the hazardous chemicals, activities, or devices that will be used.

2. Identify and assess the risks involved.

3. Describe the safety precautions and procedures that will be used to reduce the risks.

4. Describe the disposal procedures that will be used (when applicable).

5. List the source(s) of safety information.

To be completed and signed by the Designated Supervisor (or Qualified Scientist, when applic

I agree with the risk assessment and safety precautions and procedures described above. I certify that I have reviewed tl **Research Plan** and will provide direct supervision.

_____   _____   _____

Designated Supervisor's Printed Name   Signature   Date of Re
                                                                                    (must be prior to experimentation.)

_____   _____

Position & Institution   Phone or email contact information

Human Subjects Form (4)
Required for all research involving humans. IRB approval required before experimentation.

Student's Name_____

Title of Project_____

To be completed by Student Researcher in collaboration with the Designated Supervisor/Qualified Sci
(All questions must be answered; additional page may be attached.)

1) Describe the purpose of this study and list all of the research procedures in which the subject will be involved. Inclu   the duration of the subject's involvement. Attach any survey or questionnaire.

2) Describe and assess any potential risk or discomfort, and, if any, potential benefits (physical, psychological, social,   gal or other) that may be reasonably expected by participating in this research.

3) Describe the procedures that will be used to minimize risk, to obtain informed consent and/or assent, and to maintai   dential-
ity.

For questions or concerns regarding this research, contact: _____ at _____
                                                                    Adult Sponsor   Email/phone

To be completed by Institutional Review Board (IRB) <u>prior</u> to experimentation: Determination of risk, including physical and psychological risks (See risk evaluation, p. 14.)

[ ] **Minimal risk where informed consent is recommended, but not required.** Justification for waiver of informed consent for research
with subjects under 18 years of age:_____

[ ] **Minimal risk where informed consent is REQUIRED.**

[ ] **More than minimal risk where informed consent & a Qualified Scientist are REQUIRED**

IRB SIGNATURES (All three signatures are required)
1) Medical Professional: *(MUST circle one)* (a psychologist, psychiatrist, medical doctor, licensed social worker, physician's asst., or registered nurse)

_____   _____   _____
Printed Name (including title)   Signature   Date of Approval
2) Science Teacher:

_____   _____   _____
Printed Name   Signature   Date of Approval
3) School Administrator:

_____   _____   _____
Printed Name   Signature   Date of Approval

To be completed by Human Subject:
(prior to experimentation)
                                 _____
                                        Printed Name

[ ] [ ] I have read and understand the conditions and risks
yes no above and I consent/assent to voluntarily participate in
         this research study.

[ ] [ ] I realize I am free to withdraw my consent and to
yes no withdraw from this study at any time without negative
         consequences.

[ ] [ ] I consent to the use of visual images (photos, videos,
yes no etc.) involving my participation in this research.

_____   _____
Signature   Date

To be completed by Parent/Guardian:
(Prior to experimentation and
when participant is under 18 and
informed consent is required)
                                 _____
                                        Printed Name

[ ] [ ] I have read and understand the conditions and risks above
yes no and consent to the participation of my child.

[ ] [ ] I have reviewed a copy of any survey or questionnaire used
yes no in the research.

[ ] [ ] I consent to the use of visual images (photos, videos, etc.)
yes no involving my child in this research.

_____   _____
Signature   Date

Vertebrate Animal Form (5A)
Required for all research involving vertebrate animals that is conducted in a Non-Regulated Research S (SRC approval required before experimentation.)

Student's Name _____

Title of Project _____

To be completed by Student Researcher:

1. Common name (or Genus, species) and number of animals used.

2. Describe completely the housing and husbandry to be provided. Include the cage/pen size, number of animals ¡ environment, bedding, type of food, frequency of food and water, how often animal is observed, etc.

3. What will happen to the animals after experimentation?

To be completed by Scientific Review Committee (SRC) PRIOR to experimentation:

☐ Observational study only. Veterinarian and Designated Supervisor NOT required.

☐ Behavioral or nutritional study. Designated Supervisor REQUIRED. Please have applicable person sign below.

☐ Behavioral or nutritional study. Veterinarian and Designated Supervisor REQUIRED. Please have applicable persons sign below.

☐ Behavioral or nutritional study. Veterinarian, Designated Supervisor and Qualified Scientist REQUIRED. Please have applicable persons sign below and complete a Qualified Scientist Form (2).

The SRC has carefully reviewed this study and finds it is an appropriate study and may be conducted in a non-regulated researc site.

SRC Pre-Approval Signature:

_____   _____   _____
SRC Chair Printed Name   Signature   Date of Approval

To be completed by Veterinarian:

☐ I certify that I have reviewed this research and animal husbandry with the student prior to the start of experimentation.

☐ I certify that I will provide veterinary medical and nursing care in case of illness or emergency.

_____   _____
Printed Name   Email/Phone

_____   _____
Signature   Date of Approval

To be completed by Designated Supervisor:

☐ I certify that I have reviewed this research and animal husbandry with the student prior to the start of experimentation and I accept primary responsibility for the care and handling of the animals in this project.

☐ I certify that I will directly supervise the experiment.

_____   _____
Printed Name   Email/Phone

_____   _____
Signature   Date of Approval

Vertebrate Animal Form (5B)

Required for all research involving vertebrate animals that is conducted at a Regulated Research Institut (IACUC approval required before experimentation.)

Student's Name ———————————————————————————————————————

Title of Project ———————————————————————————————————————

Title and Protocol Number of IACUC Approved Project———————————————————————

To be completed by Qualified Scientist or Principal Investigator:

1. Was this a student-generated idea or was it a subset of your work?

2. Were you made aware of the ISEF Rules before the student began experimentation?

3. What laboratory training, including dates, was provided to the student?

4. Species of animals used: ——————————————————— Number of animals us ————

5. USDA Pain Category designated for this study:

6. Describe, in detail, the role of the student in this project: procedures and equipment they were involved v provided and safety precautions employed. (Attach extra pages if necessary.)

7. Attach a copy of the Regulated Research Institution IACUC Approval. A letter from the Qualified Scientist or Principal Investigator is not sufficient.

Certification or Documentation of Student Researcher Training

———————————————————————

List Certificate Number or Attach Documentation   Date(s) of Training

———————————————————————

Qualified Scientist/Principal Investigator Printed Name Signature   Da

———————————————————————

IACUC Chair/Coordinator Printed Name Signature   Da

International Rules 2006/2007 **full text of the rules and electronic copies of forms are available at www.sciserv.org/isef**

Potentially Hazardous Biological Agents Form (6A)

Required for all research involving microorganisms, rDNA and fresh tissue, blood and body fl
SRC/IACUC/IBC approval required before experimentation.

Student's Name _____

Title of Project _____

To be completed by Student Researcher in collaboration with Qualified Scientist/Designated Supervisor:
(All questions are applicable and must be answered; additional page(s) may be attached.)

1) Identify potentially hazardous biological agents to be used in this experiment. Include the source, quantity and the biosafety level risk group of each microorganism.

2) Describe the site of experimentation including the level of biological containment.

3) Describe the method of disposal of all cultured materials and other potentially hazardous biological agents.

4) Describe the procedures that will be used to minimize risk. (personal protective equip., hood type, etc.)

5) What final biosafety level do you recommend for this project given the risk assessment you conducted?

To be completed by Qualified Scientist or Designated Supervisor

1) What training did the student receive for this project?

2) Do you concur with the biosafety information and recommendation provided by the student researcher above? ☐ Yes ☐ No
If no, please explain.

_____   _____   _____
QS/DS Printed Name   Signature   Date of Signature

To be completed by SRC prior to experimentation:

☐ The SRC has carefully studied this project's Research Plan and the risk level assessment above and approves this study as a BSL-1 study, which must be conducted at a BSL-1 or above laboratory.

☐ The SRC has carefully studied this project's Research Plan and the risk level assessment above and approves this study as a BSL-2 study, which must be conducted at a BSL-2 or above laboratory.

_____
SRC Chair's Printed Name

_____   _____
Signature   Date of Approval

To be completed by SRC after experimentation with Institutional pre-approval:

☐ This project was reviewed and approved by the appropriate institutional board (e.g. IACUC, IBC) before experimentation at a BSL-1 or BSL-2 laboratory and complies with the ISEF rules. The required institutional forms are attached.

_____
SRC Chair's Printed Name

_____   _____
Signature   Date of Approval

Human and Vertebrate Animal Tissue Form (6B)

Required for all projects using fresh tissue, primary cell cultures, blood, blood products and body fluids
If the research involves living organisms, please ensure that the proper human or animal forms are completed.
ALL PROJECTS USING ANY TISSUE LISTED ABOVE, MUST ALSO COMPLETE FORM 6A.

Student's Name _____

Title of Project _____

To be completed by Student Researcher:

1) What tissue(s), organ(s), or part(s) will be used?

2) Where will the above tissue, organ, or part be obtained (identify each separately):

3) If the tissue is obtained from a source within a research institution, please provide information regarding t
   study from which the tissue was obtained. Include the name of the research institution, the title of the study, the
   IACUC approval number and date of IACUC approval.

To be completed by the Designated Supervisor or Qualified Scientist:

☐ I verify that the student will work solely with organs, tissues, cultures or cells that will be supplied to him/her
   by myself or qualified personnel from the laboratory; and that if vertebrate animals were euthanized they were
   euthanized for a purpose other than the student's research.

AND/OR

☐ I certify that the blood, blood products, tissues or body fluids in this project will be handled in accordance with
   the standards and guidance set forth in Occupational Safety and Health Act, 29CFR, Subpart Z, 1910.1030 -
   Blood Borne Pathogens.

_____   _____   _____
Printed Name   Signature   Date Signed
                                                        (Must be prior to experimentation.)

_____   _____
Title   Phone or email contact information

_____
Institution

Continuation Projects Form (7)
Required for projects that are a continuation in the same field of study as a previous project.
This form should be accompanied by the previous year's abstract, Form (1A) and Research Plan.

Student's Name _____

To be completed by Student Researcher:

List all components of the current project that make it new and different from previous research. Use an addi
2003 and earlier projects.

Components	Current Research Project	Previous Research Project
1. Title		2005-2006: 2004-2005:
2. Objectives		2005-2006: 2004-2005:
3. Variables studied		2005-2006: 2004-2005:
4. Line of investigation		2005-2006: 2004-2005:
5. Additional changes		2005-2006: 2004-2005:

*This form must be displayed at your project to help provide the judges a better
understanding of your project and what research has been done in the current year.*

I hereby certify that the above information is correct and that the current year Abstract & Certification a
project display board properly reflect work done only in the current year.

_____   _____   _____
Student's Printed Name   Signature   Date of Signature

Information on Required Abstract & Certification for ALL Projects at the Intel ISEF
* This form may not be relevant for your regional or state fair; please refer to instructions from your affiliated fair. *

In ADDITION to the basic form requirements for ALL Projects and any other requirements due to specific areas of research, Abstract & Certification is required at the conclusion of research. Details on this requirement follow.

Completing the Abstract

After finishing research and experimentation, you are required to write a (maximum) 250 word, one-page abstract. This should be written on the Official Abstract and Certification Form as provided by Science Service. The abstract **should include:**

a) *purpose of the experiment*
b) *procedures used,*
c) *data, and*
d) *conclusions.*

It may also include any possible research applications. Only minimal reference to previous work may be included. An abstract **should not include**:

a) *acknowledgments (including naming the research institution and/ or mentor with which you were working), or*
b) *work or procedures done by the mentor.*

Completing the Certification

At the bottom of the Abstract & Certification form there are five questions. Please read each carefully, answer appropriately, and sign in the signature box to certify your answers. The Intel ISEF Scientific Research Committee will review and approve the abstract and answers to the questions.

Revisions or questions will be resolved via an SRC appointment on site at the Intel ISEF. Please bring a copy of your Abstract & Certification to the fair. Only after final Intel ISEF SRC approval has been obtained via a stamped/embossed copy of this Abstract & Certification may a Finalist make copies to hand out to the judges and the public.

Intel ISEF SAMPLE ABSTRACT & CERTIFICATION

TITLE
Finalist's Name
School Name, City and State, Country

Start Typing the Body of Your Abstract Here Beginning at the Left Margin

Category
Pick one only--
mark an "X" in
box at right

Animal Sciences ☐
Behavioral and Social Science ☐
Biochemistry ☐
Cellular & Molecular Biology ☐
Chemistry ☐
Computer Science ☐
Earth Science ☐
Eng. Materials & Bioengineering ☐
Eng.: Electrical & Mechanical ☐
Energy & Transportation ☐
Environmental Analysis ☐
Environmental Management ☐
Mathematical Sciences ☐
Medicine and Health ☐
Microbiology ☐
Physics & Astronomy ☐
Plant Sciences ☐

1. As a part of this research project, the student directly handled, manipulated, or interacted with (check all that apply): ☐ human subjects   ☐ potentially hazardous biological agents   ☐ vertebrate animals   ☐ microorganisms   ☐ rDNA   ☐ tissue

2. Student independently performed all procedures as outlined in this abstract. ☐ yes ☐ no

3. A Regulated Research Institution was a work site for some or all of this project. ☐ yes ☐ no

4. This project is a continuation. ☐ yes ☐ no

5. My display board includes photographs/visual depictions of humans (other than myself): ☐ yes ☐ no

I/We hereby certify that the above statements are correct and the information provided in the Abstract is the result of one year's research. I/We also attest that the above properly reflects my/our own work.

Finalist or Team Leader Signature   Date

FOR INTEL ISEF OFFICIAL USE ONLY

This embossed seal attests that this project is in compliance with all federal and state laws and regulations and that all appropriate reviews and approvals have been obtained including the final clearance by the Intel ISEF Scientific Review Committee.

Sample Intel ISEF Official Abstract & Certification

NOTE: Your abstract must be on the Intel International Science and Engineering Fair Abstract & Certification form and embossed/ stamped by the Intel ISEF Scientific Review Committee before it is displayed or handed out. *No pasted or taped text will be permitted.* **No other format or version of your approved Abstract & Certification will be allowed for any purpose at the Intel ISEF.**

ABSTRACT & CERTIFICATION
INSTRUCTIONS

This abstract form and the instructions below are intended for Intel ISEF finalists. Entrants of regional and state fairs may also be directed to use this form. Please follow all local, regional or state instructions. As an Intel ISEF finalist, you will receive further information and will be required to complete this abstract in an on-line abstract system immediately after winning at your regional or state fair.

WRITING REQUIREMENTS

Abstracts should be **single-spaced using 12-point type** from a black ribbon or laser cartridge. Abstracts may not exceed 250 words and must be typed within the predefined area (5.5" tall by 6" wide). Type title (Title Case required); your first name, middle initial and last name; and your school's name, city and state within the first .75 inches of space within the box. Two lines may be used for the title. *Teams must include all team member names.*

Example: Effects of Marine Engine Exhaust Water on Algae
            Mary E. Jones
            Hometown High School, Hometown, Pennsylvania

BE SURE TO ANSWER THE 4 QUESTIONS BY MARKING THE APPROPRIATE BOXES AND CERTIFY BY SIGNING

TIPS ON WRITING

The three most common reasons that a student is asked to rewrite the abstract are 1) including acknowledgements (this includes naming the research institution and/or mentor with which you were working) 2) describing research not completed by the student finalist and 3) describing research done in previous years. Please limit yourself to describing research **you** have done in the current year.

THE ABSTRACT ON YOUR DISPLAY BOARD

Because your Abstract & Certification will not be considered an official one until it is stamped/embossed at the Intel ISEF, you must NOT mount a copy of any abstract on your vertical display board before arriving at the Intel ISEF. If you plan to have an Abstract & Certification on your vertical display board (recommended), you should leave a space (8.5 by 11 inches) for it to be mounted after you have arrived at the ISEF and your Official Abstract & Certification has been returned with the embossed approval.

If you do not plan to mount a copy of your official Abstract & Certification on your vertical display board, you should bring with you a means by which to display the official Abstract & Certification in a vertical position somewhere at your project. The only abstract allowed anywhere at the Intel ISEF is the official Abstract & Certification. **The term "abstract" may NOT be used** as a title or reference for any information **on your** vertical **display board** or in readily visible materials at the project **except as a part of displaying the Official Abstract & Certification.**

Appendix C

Bibliography

A bibliography is a list of sources of written information that you used to gather background information or information for any other part of your science project. The bibliography should follow a specific format, shown below, and it should contain any reference in which you found useful material. Sources should be listed in alphabetical order. Your teacher may require a minimum number of sources in order to encourage you to look at a variety of sources.

This appendix is divided into two sections:

1. Bibliography format and examples

2. Actual bibliography for this book.

Section 1 – Bibliography format and examples

Below are some formats and examples of bibliography entries from various kinds of sources. NOTE: Your teacher may specify using formats found in the MLA Handbook or the AP Style Book, or some other formatting guide. These may differ on such matters as whether to put book and magazine titles in italics or to underline them. Internet addresses are almost always underlined simply because most word processing programs do it automatically. So check with your teacher, but also check with your local science fair organization, as they may require different formats!

FORMATS

ENCYCLOPEDIA (with an author's name given)
Author's name, "Title of article," *Name of encyclopedia*, Year

ENCYCLOPEDIA (with no author's name given)
"Title of article," *Name of encyclopedia*, Year

BOOK
Author's last name, first name, (use the Latin phrase "et al" if more than three authors), *Title of book*, Place of publication, Publisher, Year.

MAGAZINE
Author's name, "Title of article," *Name of magazine*, Volume number, Date of publication, Page numbers used.

VIDEO / TELEVISION / RADIO
"Title of episode," *Title of program*, Name of network, Local station, Broadcast date.

GOVERNMENT PAMPHLET
Name of agency publishing the information, *Title of publication*, Place of publication, Date of publication.

PERSONAL INTERVIEW
Name of person interviewed, Occupation, Place of employment, Interviewed: Date of interview.

ELECTRONIC MAIL (Email)
Author of Email message, Subject line of message, [Online] Available email: student@address.edu from author@address.edu, Date of message.

INTERNET (or) WORLD WIDE WEB (WWW)
Author, Title of item, [Online] Available http://address/filename, Date of document or download. Note: Whether or not to underline web addresses is still being debated.

USENET NEWSGROUPS
Author, Title of item, [Online] Available usenet: group, Date of post.

For other examples of how bibliography entries may be written, talk to any librarian.

EXAMPLES

Binkie, Bartholemew. "Plant Growth," *World Book Encyclopedia*, 1997.

DiStephano, Vance, Guidelines for Better Plant Growth, [Online] Available http://www.usa.net/~avanced/home/better-plant growth.html, January 9 , 1997

Farmer, Fred, Expert Gardener,Washington State University Cooperative Extension, Interviewed Sept . 8, 1996.

Heimler, Charles H., et al, *Focus On Life Science*, Colombus, Ohio, Merrill, 1984.

Kanfer, Steven. "Entre-Manure - Making money from fertilizer!" *Farm Digest*, 24 May 1993: 71.

"Photosynthesis," *Groliers Encyclopedia*, 1997

"Plants." Videotape. National Geographic Video, 1985. 60 min.

Washington Department of Tomato Growth Studies, "Growing Tomatoes in the home garden," Olympia, Wa, 1993.]

Section 2 - Actual bibliography for this book

Asimov, Isaac, *Great Ideas of Science*, Boston, Houghton Mifflin Company, 1969.

Barrow, Bruce B., "Metric system ," World Book Online Reference Centre, http://www.worldbookonline.com/ar?/na/ar/co/ar358560.htm, August 23, 2003.

Bartz, Albert E., *Basic Statistical Concepts*, 3rd Ed. New York: Macmillan Publishing, 1988.

Brown, Mike, "How to present your science project," [Online] http://www.selah.wednet.edu/JHS/Brown/howpresentproj.html#topofpresentpage, downloaded Aug. 31, 2003.

Brown, Mike, "How to use this model project journal," [Online] http://www.selah.wednet.edu/JHS/Brown/SMSProjJourn.html#topofjournal, circa 1999.

Fogt, Robert, "Online conversion," BlueSparks Network, http://www.onlineconversion.com/length_common.htm, August 23, 2003.

Haduch, Bill, *Science Fair Secrets*, New York, Dutton Children's Books, 2002.

Iritz, Maxine Haren, *Blue Ribbon Science Fair Projects*, Blue Ridge Summit, PA, Tab Books, 1991.

Johnson, Doug, "Welcome to CyberFair," http://www.isd77.k12.mn.us/resources/cf/welcome.html, Oct. 8, 2001.

Judging Guide, 43rd Alamo Regional Academy of Science and Engineering Fair, Feb. 16, 1999.

Morano, David, "Experimental science projects: An introductory level guide," [online], http://www.isd77.k12.mn.us/resources/cf/SciProjIntro.html, May 27, 1995.

Newkirk, Ken, "Re: More info about book," email dated Feb. 25, 2003 to Mike Dickinson.

Platt, John R., "Strong Inference," *Science Magazine*, Volume 146, Number 3642, October 16, 1964, pp. 347-353.

Tindell, J., "Kids Guide to Science Projects," [Online] http:edweb.tusd.k12.az.us/jtindell/check.html, downloaded Aug. 31, 2003

Tocci, Salvatore, *How to do a science project*, New York, Franklin Watts, 1997.

Wright, Orville, and Kelly, Fred C., *How We Invented the Airplane*, New York, David McKay Company, 1953.

Index

*For more information, you can also
check the website for this book:*
http://www.scienceprojecthelper.com

To order copies of this book, go to:
http://www.wingspress.com

3792